Your Horoscope 2020

....

Capricorn

Your Horoscope 2020

....

Capricorn

22nd December - 20th January

igloobooks

igloobooks

Published in 2019
by Igloo Books Ltd
Cottage Farm
Sywell
NN6 0BJ
www.igloobooks.com

0819 001.01
2 4 6 8 10 9 7 5 3 1
ISBN 978-1-78905-712-6

Written by Belinda Campbell and Jennifer Zelinger

Cover design by Dave Chapman
Edited by Bobby Newlyn-Jones

Printed and manufactured in China

CONTENTS

· · · · · · · · · · · · · · · · · · ·

INTRODUCTION
. . . .

This horoscope has been specifically created to allow
you to get the most from astrological patterns and
the way they have a bearing on not only your zodiac
sign, but nuances within it. Using the diary section
of the book you can read about the influences and
possibilities of each and every day of the year. It will
be possible for you to see when you are likely to be
cheerful and happy or those times when your nature
is in retreat and will be more circumspect. The
diary will help to give you a feel for the specific
'cycles' of astrology and the way they can subtly
change your day-to-day life.

THE CHARACTER OF THE SEA GOAT

....

One small step for Capricorn can certainly be one giant leap for mankind when this determined sign gets its teeth into something. Whether it's dreaming of the stars like Capricorns Buzz Aldrin and Stephen Hawking or striving for first place like Tiger Woods and Lewis Hamilton, Capricorns are the Earth signs of the calendar that can make their dreams a reality. Belonging to the tenth house of the zodiac calendar where careers and vocations are key, the role that a disciplined Capricorn takes on, be it in business, science, or on the stage, can take them to dizzying heights of success. As an Earth sign, tangible rewards can be essential to Capricorns, just look at their designer clothes, nice cars and beautiful houses – and if a Capricorn hasn't quite reached their goals yet, their dreams of grandeur will likely inspire them to only work harder.

Born with buckets of ambition, the Goat-symbolised Capricorn will not be satisfied with climbing mere ladders and will likely set themselves mountains to ascend. If the path they have taken is proving to be too rocky, rejection and failure can hit this prideful sign hard and any pain might be internalised due to their negative nature. Capricorns are pioneering cardinal characters, and the world can be more than happy to dance to their Pied Piper tune. Just look at Calvin Harris, a Forbes-listed Capricorn recorded for being the highest paid DJ in the world for six consecutive years, showing how hardworking Capricorns can not only reach but stay at the top of their profession. Status is of all importance to Capricorns so being top dog, or Sea Goat rather, could be what helps drive this sign to the highest peaks of their success. Their top-of-the-podium seeking attitude is perhaps why the number one and number two spots for the record amount of Formula 1 wins are both held by Capricorns, Michael Schumacher and Lewis Hamilton. Whatever their goals are, with authoritative Saturn ruling over Capricorn, this disciplined sign is sure to get results.

THE SEA GOAT

Often depicted as a mountain Goat with the tail of a fish, Capricorns are the practical and creative doers of the zodiac calendar. With the surefooted hooves of the Goat, Capricorns can approach their goals with perseverance and authority whilst their fishy tail suggests that they may also have a creative and sensitive side hiding beneath their stoic features. Earth sign Capricorns will usually find comfort in solid things and enjoy following a clear path that has tangible rewards at the end of it. This Goat isn't about taking the easy route though, Capricorns can be found confidently scaling the trickiest and longest paths with their stubbornly hardworking attitude. Born at the start of winter, the Goat is happy to take the path less trodden and seek out their own way in life, which can give them a reputation being a loner to some extent. The Goat can be a serious soul thanks to their authoritative planet of Saturn so would do well to try and lighten up from time to time and remember what it was like to be a kid again.

SATURN

The second largest planet in the Solar System, Saturn rules over the eye-catching Capricorn. Dead set on achieving their goals, this ground-breaking Earth sign is likely to be well known in whatever they choose to do in their lives. Named after the Roman god of agriculture, Saturn led Capricorns can be wonderful at sowing a seed, working the earth and watching the abundant fruits of their labour grow to fruition. Despite Saturday being the namesake of Capricorn's ruling planet, this Saturn sign can struggle to say goodbye to their work and hello to the weekend. The planet of authority and discipline might not make Saturn an obvious choice for kicking off a fun-filled weekend, however, it is a forced reminder that breaks must be taken and marks a tradition that even this sign can't ignore. For Capricorns, taking time away from their work can be tough so their ruling planet, Saturn, can act as an important reminder that all work and no play makes Capricorn as useful as a dull blade.

ELEMENTS, MODES AND POLARITIES

Each sign is made up of a unique combination of three defining groups: elements, modes and polarities. Each of these defining parts can manifest in good and bad ways, and none should be seen to be a positive or a negative – including the polarities! Just like a jigsaw puzzle, piecing these groups together can help illuminate why each sign has certain characteristics and help us find a balance.

ELEMENTS

Fire: Dynamic and adventurous, signs with Fire in them can be extroverted. Others are naturally drawn to them because of the positive light they give off, as well as their high levels of energy and confidence.

Earth: Signs with the Earth element are steady and driven with their ambitions. They make for a solid friend, parent or partner due to their grounded influence and nurturing nature.

Air: The invisible element that influences each of the other elements significantly, Air signs will provide much-needed perspective to others with their fair thinking, verbal skills and key ideas.

Water: Warm in the shallows and freezing as ice. This mysterious element is essential to the growth of everything around it, through its emotional depth and empathy.

MODES

Cardinal: Pioneers of the calendar, cardinal signs jump-start each season and are the energetic go-getters.

Fixed: Marking the middle of the calendar, fixed signs firmly denote and value steadiness and reliability.

Mutable: As the seasons end, the mutable signs adapt and give themselves over gladly to the promise of change.

POLARITIES

Positive: Typically extroverted, positive signs take physical action and embrace outside stimulus in their life.

Negative: Usually introverted, negative signs value emotional development and experiencing life from the inside out.

CAPRICORN IN BRIEF

The table below shows the key attributes of Capricorn. Use it for quick reference and to understand more about this fascinating sign.

SYMBOL	RULING PLANET	MODE	ELEMENT	HOUSE
♑	♄	∧	▽	Ⅹ
The Sea Goat	Saturn	Cardinal	Earth	Tenth

COLOUR	BODY PART	POLARITY	GENDER	POLAR SIGN
		⊖	♀	♋
Brown	Joints, Bones and Teeth	Negative	Feminine	Cancer

LOVE

. . . .

Despite Capricorn's fishy tail suggesting a sensitive side seen in Water signs, it's unlikely that this Earth sign will feel all that comfortable with emotional displays of affection. When a Capricorn wants to express to their other half just how much they mean to them, it may be by way of physical gifts, like a box of expensive chocolates or even a new car. The greatest romantic gift for a Capricorn will usually be an engagement ring, as marriage will be essential to many of this sign, partly due to their desire for security and their value of upholding tradition. Giving a partner emotional support and stability can be essential in any relationship, however, for the pragmatic Capricorn who can be too focused on providing financial security for their loved ones, this can at times be forgotten. If a Capricorn is in the habit of showing their love by ways of expensive present giving, they should remember that gifts of the greatest value do not always have the highest price tags.

Born in the tenth house in the zodiac calendar that focuses on careers and vocation, a Capricorn can be guilty of prioritising their work above their relationship. For a Capricorn, they may view the long hours that they are spending at the office as a sacrifice that they are happy to make for their partner in order to provide them with a beautiful home, money for holidays, or expensive cars. Whilst a Capricorn is unlikely to be deliberately neglecting their partner, usually being highly devoted in their relationships, establishing a balance between home life and work life can be essential to Capricorns finding long-term happiness in love. Finding a playful partner that can coax this Goat sign out from their desk of solitude and persuade them to relax and enjoy life is key for Capricorns in love.

ARIES: COMPATIBILITY 1/5

The cynical Capricorn is not an obvious lover for ambitious Aries but shouldn't necessarily be ruled out entirely as a potential partner. Capricorns usually take longer to make up their mind about a partner than the quick-working Aries, so Aries will need to exert some patience and work at Capricorn's slower pace if they want this challenging relationship to work. Like with any relationships, their differences can be their strengths. Be mindful of not wanting to change each other and learn how each can make the other a better, more well-rounded, person.

TAURUS: COMPATIBILITY 3/5

Capricorn and Taurus in love are loyal and true to each other. These two Earth signs value hard work and are driven by their need to enjoy the fruits of their labours. The home that these two could build together will likely be full of beautiful and expensive objects, with a couple of prized cars jewelling their garage. Whilst both will have dreams of marriage, Capricorn is the more traditional one and will probably approach the subject first. Taurus should try to inject joy and fun into the relationship to teach Capricorn to enjoy the lighter side of life.

GEMINI: COMPATIBILITY 1/5

This Earth and Air coupling between Capricorn and Gemini may be an unlikely match but awareness of their differences could help create a stronger bond. Capricorns appreciate the tangible: a good career and beautiful home, whilst Geminis love exciting ideas and the invisible workings of the mind. Whilst a Gemini's mutable element fits well with the cardinal aspect of Capricorn, what drives Capricorn may be at odds with the interests of Gemini. This polar opposite couple, Capricorn negative and Gemini positive, may struggle to find common ground but could stand to learn the most from one another.

CANCER: COMPATIBILITY 5/5

Opposites on the zodiac calendar, Capricorn and Cancer can experience a tenacious love. When Water sign Cancer rains down on Earth sign Capricorn they can create a beautiful life together. Symbolised often with a fish's tail, the Sea Goat that represents Capricorn can swim happily in a Cancerian's warm waters. A Cancerian can indeed help coax a playfulness in Capricorn that others don't always see. Capricorns are ruled by the authoritative planet of Saturn so could be a strong parenting partner for the family orientated Cancerian. If these two hardworking signs fall in love with each other, the dedication that they share could be staggering.

LEO: COMPATIBILITY 4/5

Leo and Capricorn are the success story of when
opposites can attract in love. Both these signs tend
to have a clear sense of purpose, for Leo it is in their
personal life goals and for Capricorn a clear career
path is their focus. Leo Barack Obama and Capricorn
Michelle Obama are an ideal example of how well
these two can work towards achieving their dreams
together. Capricorn can show Leo what hard work can
accomplish, and Leo can bring the fun that sometimes
the cool and dignified Capricorn can be lacking. Leo
and Capricorn are two strong characters that can be
even stronger together.

VIRGO: COMPATIBILITY 4/5

When the hardworking Capricorn and meticulous
Virgo fall in love, there won't be many cracks in their
relationship. With a Virgo's toolkit of organisation and
practical skills and a Capricorn's portfolio of material
achievements, this hardworking couple may be great at
taking on exciting and grand projects together. Perhaps
building their own home somewhere in the countryside
would suit this couple, where their shared Earth
element can be appreciated at its best, and their quieter
negative energies embraced. This firm relationship may
lack some spontaneity, so thoughtful surprises now and
again could help keep their home fires burning.

LIBRA: COMPATIBILITY 1/5

The firm footed Goat of Capricorn and high-spirited Air sign of Libra could have little shared ground and struggle to strike a balance in love, but a relationship should not be ruled out. Born in the seventh house of relationships, Libras may struggle if Capricorns, born in the tenth house of careers, put their job before their partnership, so striking a balance between work and personal life will be essential for a happy union. It could be hard to find equality for this Earth and Air match when their differences are so vast, however, their commitment could well outweigh any differences.

SCORPIO: COMPATIBILITY 5/5

When Capricorn and Scorpio set their sights on each other, these highly dedicated signs could be in it for the long run. Placed two apart on the zodiac calendar, theirs is a devout bond that is likely to be highly compatible with matching negative energies, complementary elements, and strong cardinal and fixed modes. A Capricorn can offer the security that Scorpio desires and Scorpio can be the powerful influence that feeds Capricorn's ambition. Scorpio will bring the fun and Capricorn will bring the itinerary to go with it. If they can take it in turns to rule the roost, their love could go the distance.

SAGITTARIUS: COMPATIBILITY 2/5

A materialist Capricorn and dazzling Sagittarius can both be guilty of feeling a little superior, which won't do in a partnership, especially when these two can have such different approaches to life. The rational Capricorn may be fearful of going to daring heights with their lively Sagittarius partner but if they are open to Sagittarian's optimism, they could learn to love more bravely. A Sagittarius may feel constrained by Capricorn's constant reminder that actions have consequences but looking before they leap could be a vital lesson that a Capricorn teaches their Sagittarian partner. The key to their happiness may be embracing each other's opposites.

CAPRICORN: COMPATIBILITY 3/5

Through better and through worse, there's probably no peak that these two Goats could not reach together. When a cardinal couple like two Capricorns fall in love, their accomplishments can be great, however, arguments over who is the driver in this relationship can cause rifts. Like any long journey or long-term relationship, it's all about taking turns behind the wheel; someone should remember to bring the car games as fun may be forgotten by this serious pair. Both Earth signs, these two may be focused on material things but they are also devoted and grounded partners to one another.

AQUARIUS: COMPATIBILITY 1/5

Both ruled by Saturn, Capricorns and Aquarians will usually have a good understanding of the rules of love, however, Aquarians are co-ruled by Uranus so may rebel against the traditions that most Capricorns value. A Capricorn and an Aquarius can both be extremely independent people which may be what attracts them to one another, and as a creative couple they can really bring out the best in each other. This is a union of strong personalities and beliefs that may struggle to find common ground due to their opposite negative and positive energies, although their differences and determination could be their success.

PISCES: COMPATIBILITY 3/5

An Earth and Water love is bound to be a complementary match, and the relationship with a Capricorn and Piscean may be about helping each other grow as individuals and flourish as a couple. Capricorn will bring a practical mind and an active spirit with their cardinal nature whilst the mutable Piscean will provide compassion and teach their Goat to be flexible. Both sides can retreat into themselves in times of great focus or reflection, particularly Pisceans if their Goat partner is being overbearing. However, their matching negative energies could form a deep emotional connection with each other and demonstrate true patience and dedication.

FAMILY AND FRIENDS

Capricorns are the hard workers of the zodiac calendar, and a big driving force as to why they work so hard can be their family. A Capricorn may have ambitions of being the provider to their loved ones, providing food on the table, money for school trips, and a nice roof over their heads. Capricorns are usually house-proud individuals and for good reason, with their traditional taste and appreciation of materials, their house may have original beam features or luxurious sofas that show off their love for sturdy and tangible objects. Building a solid and secure homelife for their family may be a Capricorn's dream and their self-sufficiency and drive can make them determined not to rely on others. Capricorns should be careful of becoming too focused on their work life and neglecting their home life as they might find that they start to alienate themselves from their loved ones if they do so. Sharing responsibilities will free them up to enjoy the fruits of their labours and the real treasures in their life, which for homebody Capricorn is truly their family.

Like everything else in a Capricorn's life, friendships too may be measured by their value. For some cool kids, this cardinal Goat sign may seek out friendships that they believe will advance their social status further, as is their talent for sniffing out a solid investment. Whilst Capricorns love having control over their destiny, this sign would do well to leave the strategising in their financial lives, and out of their friendships if they don't want to get a reputation of using people for their own personal gain. When Capricorns take a day off from planning their empires, they may find that the unexpected or oldest friendships this sign has are the most rewarding and worth investing more time in. Capricorns are a steady force of friendship, ready to support their loved ones through good times and bad. But they may not always be as receptive to help from their friends. Positive and high energy signs like Leo and Sagittarius can help Capricorns loosen up and learn to not just live life to its maximum but to have fun whilst doing so too.

As a child, parents can be the first and key figure of authority in most people's lives, however, for Saturn ruled Capricorn, their first experience of discipline and establishing boundaries can be even more relevant. Should a Capricorn have their own children, or look after other people's children, their Saturn influence will mean that their deep-set feelings of responsibility may make them a strict parent or guardian as they will not take these duties lightly. Setting curfews, dishing out chores, and checking homework could be jobs that the Capricorn parent takes in their stride. Capricorns may also want to teach their child practical skills like learning to drive or riding a bike and will no doubt take huge pride in witnessing and being part of their children's achievements.

MONEY AND CAREERS

. . . .

Being a certain star sign will not dictate the type of
career that you have, although the characteristics that
fall under each sign could help you identify the areas
in which you could potentially thrive. Conversely, to
succeed in the workplace, it is just as important to
understand what you are good at as it is to know what
you are less brilliant at so that you can see the areas
in which you will need to perhaps work harder in to
achieve your career and financial goals.

Belonging to the tenth house where occupation and
vocation are everything, it is no wonder that this sign
has a great chance of rising up the ranks in their chosen
profession. As a cardinal sign ruled by the authoritative
planet of Saturn, Capricorns can suit high-powered and
high-earning jobs as a director or CEO of a company.
Ambition is Capricorn's middle name and thanks to
their cardinal nature, their drive for success can see
them become trailblazers in their professional field.
Trendsetter designer Diane von Fürstenburg, activist
leader Martin Luther King Jr, and pioneer of glam rock
David Bowie are all Capricorns that have lit the way
for others to follow by climbing their personal ladders
to success. Whatever this Sea Goat sets their mind to,
Capricorn's tenacity teamed with their strong will means
that whilst they may take a while getting wherever they
are going, their destination will be worth it. They will
not be afraid of being different, nor will they apologise

for forging new paths - Capricorns know who they are and where they wany to be, so work hard to achieve their goals.

Capricorns are one of the Earth signs of the zodiac, so tangible objects can bring this sign great satisfaction. Certificates, trophies and medals will usually adorn Capricorns' walls, shelves and neck, as a visual reminder of the greatness that they can achieve. Careers where a Capricorn can use their practical skills, perhaps as a property developer or learning a specific trade may suit this sign as it could satisfy their need for material things and provide them with a solid outcome and income from their hard work. Capricorns are usually careful with money, apart from when they are trying to impress someone, in which cases they may be caught spending beyond their means in order to try and make a good impression. Whilst Capricorns may be seen to splurge, any expenses that this sign makes will be judged on what they will receive in return, so a Capricorn will probably view their spending more as investing. The returns may not always be monetary, but Capricorns will value appreciation of their gifts.

Whilst you can't always choose who you work with, it can be advantageous to learn about colleagues' key characteristics through their star signs to try and work out the best ways of working with them. Like Capricorns, Virgos can be wonderful planners, so these to-do list lovers could very well be responsible for overseeing the Christmas work do or co-presenting at important meetings together, managing projects with precision and panache. Taureans can work doggedly with hard-working Capricorns through the most difficult of tasks, and will bond over their shared grit and determination to see taks through to the end even if the odds seem to be against them. Capricorn's cardinal nature can mean that they are happy to work on their own and may clash with other cardinal signs in a contest for power, however, inspiring Aries and passionate Cancerians can make for stimulating cardinal colleagues.

HEALTH AND
WELLBEING
....

When you are as adept at climbing so many ladders in
life, overcoming obstacles and conquering mountains
like the Goat in Capricorn is, you may also find that you
have the legs for great physical challenges. Running
marathons, cycling on rocky terrains, or mountaineering
could all be challenges the sporty Capricorn enjoys, and
if there is a shiny medal or trophy to be won at the end
of it, then all the better for this magpie sign. Associated
with joints and bones, Capricorns may like to pay extra
attention to looking after these areas of the body. So
once this mountain Goat has picked up their medals for
their sporting achievements, taking the time to unwind
with some yoga stretches will no doubt help keep their
tired joints from seizing up on them. Eating a balanced
diet rich in omega-3 from plenty of fish and nuts could
help keep joints loose and well-oiled whilst taking
relevant supplements could also put the pep back into a
Capricorn's step.

Capricorns can be oh-so serious, worrying about this
or that and planning everything within an inch of its
life so that they achieve the staggering excellence that
they are after. But striving for success, whilst being a
motivational force, can at times be a tough burden to
bear, particularly if a Capricorn's dreams aren't going
to plan. This sign can have a reputation for being
pessimistic in their pragmatic approach to life, and their
grumbling can lead to moaning which can leave them

with a cold and hard view of the world. Indeed, when life gives Capricorn lemons, the severe disappointment that they are left with can make it hard to see how exactly they can make lemonade. For a sign that likes to feel surefooted, not knowing where they stand can rattle this sign and leave them feeling unsteady and uneasy. Control might not be an easy thing for Capricorns to let go of, but the sooner this sign accepts that certain things cannot be predicted, the sooner they can relax and enjoy the unknown.

Keeping Capricorn's health and wellbeing in check may be linked to keeping their work and personal life balanced. Too often, a Capricorn can put their work duties ahead of their health and happiness by working themselves to the bone on a regular basis. A Capricorn may feel better initially by staying late in the office or answering work emails at the weekend as a way of staying on top of their heavy workloads, however, working endlessly is not sustainable for any sign and a burnout could be just around the corner if this sign is not careful. Capricorns' work ethics can be admirable, but they can be so fixed on their end goal that they may not see that the journey is damaging their health and wellbeing. The key for Capricorns may be to rest just as hard as they work, as all work and no downtime is never good for any sign.

Capricorn

....

2020
DIARY PAGES

JANUARY

....

Wednesday 1st

Happy New Year Capricorn! Your start in 2020 is very communicative, and you are in an excellent mood. 2020 is one of the more crucial years for you, as there is lots of energy working in your sign continuously, so the impact will be profound. Are you ready for the ride?

Thursday 2nd

Day two this year and already Mercury is in conjunction with Jupiter in your sign. You might have a big revelation about yourself as your thoughts expand far more extensively than they have before. It is also possible that it is too much for you to begin with. Give yourself some time.

Friday 3rd

Mars is spending the final day in your area of friends and social circles so this might be a day to spend some active time with others, but it is also possible that actions lead to conflict if they are not committed. You are asked to use your energy and resources wisely.

Saturday 4th

Mars is moving into your 12th house of introspection, spirituality and retreat. You are asked to use your energy for reflecting and internal processes. Reflection is necessary to keep up with all the change. Make good use of this time, as it will allow you to find new faith and hope.

Sunday 5th

A joyful Sunday is awaiting you, the energy is harmonious, and you start best with a delicious breakfast that has a sense of luxury. You want to express yourself today so do things you love, and that connect you to earth, celebrate life and represent value for you.

Monday 6th

Monday morning and the Moon is connecting to Pluto and your planetary ruler Saturn. You are able to fulfil your duties with love. Something is in the woods though. Stick to your routines and avoid clashes of power. The next week, at least, is about to be intense.

Tuesday 7th

Saturn, your personal planet, and Pluto, the transformer and alchemist, are conjunct in your area of self, your persona and individuality. These two don't meet too often: just once in about 38 years. This could be a total makeover of your persona, a shift in how people perceive you and how you express yourself.

Wednesday 8th

You are focused on getting your chores done. Venus is currently travelling in your second house so you have a taste for extraordinary possessions and it is possible you go out and buy something that others might view as unusual. For you, it just underlines your uniqueness.

Thursday 9th

You are quite busy and struggle to reconcile. Too many different tasks demand your attention, and it is harder to focus than usual. With Venus lending you a hand you might find some extravagant solutions, so at least it won't get boring. Later today you just want some chill time with your partner.

Friday 10th

Happy Full Moon Lunar eclipse in Cancer. Quite a biggie for you, as it is happening in your area of self and the way you are seen by others. So what do your partner and other one-to-one relationships reflect back to you? With Mercury in the heart of the Sun in your sign, this can bring you amazing insights over time.

Saturday 11th

Uranus, planet of rebellion, revolution and sudden events changes direction and moves direct. So you can move ahead with your creative endeavours while your relationships mirror your current transformation of yourself. Try to observe or even better, feel your way into it. What is nurturing you?

Sunday 12th

You prefer to show and reveal yourself in an intimate setting and with the Moon in Leo you might do that today. There might be an experience you have that is difficult to grasp, but on the other hand, it allows you to see clearly why you are transforming so much.

Monday 13th

Talk about intensity Capricorn! The Sun is now joining the meeting of Saturn and Pluto, and that is shedding all the light on this new cycle of transformation. It will be most intense for those of you having their birthday today. Happy Birthday and know that something new is awaiting you!

Tuesday 14th

Venus is now in Pisces, and you focus much more on communication, short distance travel, and your neighbourhood. The Moon is in Virgo so you might feel torn between the travel bug calling from far away and Venus saying that close is far enough. You might be a little more into far distances for today.

Wednesday 15th

Your beliefs always need to stand the test of reality, and they need to align with your sense of self. You can reach a good understanding of your views concerning your personality even throughout all the shifts and changes. Try not to be too hard on yourself.

Thursday 16th

The focus is on work and what do you love more than that? Venus is making an excellent connection to Uranus so your new found self-expression might support you in your immediate environment. This could be a surprise. You weren't sure your unique approach was appreciated.

Friday 17th

Mercury enters your house of Money while the Moon is in square to the Sun. It is an excellent time to analyse your money-mindset and your shopping behaviour. You might also think about what is of value. Tension can arise at work so you want to find a solution that works for everybody.

Saturday 18th

The Moon is in your area of friendship and social circles and makes an easy connection to Venus. It is a beautiful day to invite your friends and have a gathering. If you want to throw your birthday party, this is a fantastic day to do it.

Sunday 19th

You need an honest and truthful connection to your friends, and in a conversation, some things could come up that help you to reflect on yourself and the changes and transformation you are going through. Go for the in-depth talk today and leave the superficial for some other time.

Monday 20th

You might feel a little lost today but still have the feeling you need to take some action. If you are unclear what this action can be, take the opportunity to meditate and make time for yourself. This might not be the action you considered, but it allows you to receive clarity.

Tuesday 21st

The Sun has now entered your area of money, and it is now the time of year to have a serious and honest look at your financial situation, contemplating your values as well as your sense of self-worth. Use the next thirty days to analyse your current status.

Wednesday 22nd

The Moon is in your sign Capricorn so you will likely feel comfortable, nobody else can handle all this Capricorn energy better than you. You can be the bastion of calm for others around you, who find the power too tough. Show your leading skills but don't forget to add compassion.

Thursday 23rd

The Sun squaring Uranus is up for surprises. Expect the unexpected is today's motto and with the Moon hugging Jupiter you could save the day again. The other possibility is that you are the reason for the unexpected happening to others, and they might overreact to this.

Friday 24th

Happy New Moon in Aquarius. You have the opportunity to plant a seed regarding your money and values. Have a look at what you want to invest in this year and write a list, so you know what you are saving for. Defining the goal supports getting there.

Saturday 25th

You might face some personal beliefs regarding your money-mindset. If you want to change them, affirmations and meditations can work well for you. Other than that you might be confronted with a stranger who allows you to examine your belief structures or offers unexpected help and support.

Sunday 26th

Mind and emotion are in alignment and you feel quite comfortable with the things you own. There is most often a quirky aspect to your possessions, and you are not keen on ordinary. Regarding a significant purchase, you will likely stick with today's decision, which is not always the case.

Monday 27th

Communication can be difficult today as there is a strong emphasis on Pisces energy. It is not a day to roll up your sleeves, but instead, go with the flow and delay all important conversations and meetings. It is a good day to dream away.

Tuesday 28th

The dreamy energy continues, and it is an excellent time to receive a message through your dreams. Allow yourself to go easy until noon. In the afternoon the energy shifts, and you will naturally feel pushed to get things going again. Going with the flow is a good thing to try anyway.

Wednesday 29th

Now you are back in the game, getting stuff done. The only thing that could possibly distract you is your family and their demands, which can be quite upsetting for you. Make sure you conserve your energy for what is really important and avoid unnecessary conflict.

Thursday 30th

You feel challenged by finding equilibrium between yourself and your relationship. You might feel triggered by a situation from your past, but what is actually reacting is your inner child. What can you do for your inner child to feel nurtured and cared for, how can you stand up for it?

Friday 31st

Your upbringing is one of the pieces that helped you to become the person you now are. Sometimes it is time to leave the old story behind and transform parts of yourself. Which aspect can be turned into a better version? What story will you stop telling yourself?

FEBRUARY

....

Saturday 1st

This Saturday you want to enjoy life, have some fun and
enjoy the physical pleasures of this world. Be prepared
to change your plans as you might want to go for Indian
food and end up in a steakhouse. Seek the connection to
nature as this grounding vibe just calms you down.

Sunday 2nd

Venus is in an easy connection to Pluto which means
you can find harmony and appreciation from siblings or
your immediate surroundings. This, in the end, allows
you to experience deeper healing of the outcast energy
you are sometimes feeling. Make sure to focus on having
some fun today.

Monday 3rd

Mercury is as fast as it can be and is just rushing through
your money house. It's likely you had lots of thoughts
but have not taken action yet. No worries, it is a good day
to do something practical, and the Sun is still shining a
light on this sector so you can bring in some changes.

Tuesday 4th

Mercury is joining Venus in your area of communication, siblings and surroundings. You will spend a while processing this area of life and might find a new way to communicate. Today calls for a sense of structure and discipline, but paired with compassion that you can lack at other times.

Wednesday 5th

Currently, your focus is more inward which you do not like particularly. Your beliefs and the need to retreat and connect spiritually are in conflict with your sense of practicality and handling multiple tasks at once. Use the time to focus inwards as there will be enough practical activity throughout this year.

Thursday 6th

The Moon in Cancer illuminates your relationships, and you feel the strong need to connect lovingly with your partner. You can find and give much nurturing and love today, and the two of you might not even need to talk but just enjoy some hugs and kisses.

Friday 7th

Venus is on her last day in Pisces, and you should enjoy this energy in some way, whether it's by singing or writing a poem. Emotions are intense, and it feels like a busy day as different needs are experienced throughout the day. Focus on love and compassion, and you will handle it well.

Saturday 8th

It is a beautiful day for a love letter or any declaration
of love. You are willing to open up your innermost self to
your partner and they had better be ready to acknowledge
that. Venus is now entering your area of home and family,
so this can be a time to beautify your home.

Sunday 9th

Happy Full Moon in Leo! It is a Full Moon that can
illuminate beautiful resources, and your self-love
is one of them. It is also possible that someone will
show up with some money or other resources for you,
quite literally. You have no problem with receiving if
the source is trustworthy.

Monday 10th

Your focus is on helping others, but your ego could get
in the way. You might feel that you do not have enough
ability or might feel limited in your freedom. It might
not be easy for you to get it done today, but as you would
never give up, you keep trying.

Tuesday 11th

Responsibility and structure, as well as the expansion of
your mind, all come to your aid in continuing with your
self-imposed task of helping others. There is something
you love about charity and supporting others, even
though from time to time you lack compassion.

Wednesday 12th

Your partner is likely not seeing much of you these days as you are too involved in your public and work endeavours. You enjoy it mostly, it just depends on your partner whether it backfires. You could also neglect your own needs, so conserve your energy!

Thursday 13th

It is likely today that you give more than you have, or work way over time. You might also feel the urge to stretch the rules and make sure that no power is misused. Should you sense that something is hiding in the bushes, trust your feelings and start to investigate.

Friday 14th

Happy Valentines! It is an interesting Valentines, and you might want to suggest making it Pal-entines and spend the evening not only with your partner but a couple friends, or as singles on a ladies' or gents' get-together. Why not tell your friends that you love them today?

Saturday 15th

While you start the weekend you might feel that it is more difficult to communicate reasonably. Mercury is slowing down and while moving through Pisces needs a whole different approach to communication, but you are used to that energy. Try and express yourself artistically.

Sunday 16th

Mars is entering your own sign, a place he loves to be. Throughout this transit, he will provide you with an extra oomph of energy. You will have maximum determination, and it will be easy to take up any challenge coming your way. You could be too egocentric and hard on yourself and others.

Monday 17th

Mercury starts its retrograde motion just after Mars enters your sign. This might prevent you from being too demanding on others but could also lead to misunderstandings. Be very aware and conscious of your words. You can find pleasure in writing or reading poems and receive information through your dreams.

Tuesday 18th

Jupiter, the planet of expansion, is in a beautiful connection to Neptune. With their forces combined, you can explore unknown territory and expand existing boundaries. Stay away from alcohol as there is a chance you ignore your limits with this energy. Reading or seeing a fairytale is something you might enjoy.

Wednesday 19th

The universe seems to be allowing you some compensation for this dynamic energy that Mars is providing. The Sun is entering Pisces too so it might be easy for you to be compassionate and connect to the more significant needs in your immediate surroundings. This helps you to thrive.

Thursday 20th

You can reap the rewards of something you have been working on for a while. You will feel secure and prosperous. You might want to think about how you can get to the next stage with this project but be sure not to make it about you, instead be of service to others.

Friday 21st

The thriving energy of Mars can lead to unusual manifestations of self-expression today. Be mindful how you use your power and be aware that you can create and manifest amazing and worthy things. With Uranus involved there can always be an unexpected twist, but it is likely to be in your favour.

Saturday 22nd

With the Moon in Aquarius while the Sun is in an easy connection to Uranus, you can invoke your inner genius. Worth, value and self-love are the keywords related here. It might just be about celebrating yourself for your inner genius or creating something extraordinary.

Sunday 23rd

Happy New Moon in Pisces. You might want to drift away and peace out today. It is weird enough for you to feel like this so why not go with the flow and write down your dreams while you are in this imaginative state. No need to be concerned, appreciate the experience.

Monday 24th

Venus has a passionate discussion with Jupiter. So you might need to guard yourself and defend yourself in an argument that is related to your family. You could tend to make this discussion much more significant than it has to be, maybe don't take yourself too seriously, just for once.

Tuesday 25th

Remember the summer of 2018? That was the last time Mars crossed the south node. We all enjoyed it and did things we thought were great but ended up regretting. The good news is that this time Mars passes only once so make a wise and firm decision on what you want to let go and leave it behind.

Wednesday 26th

Today's advice is to delay necessary decisions and stick with tasks you are so familiar with you could do them while you are sleeping. Mercury hugs the Sun while retrograde, and in Pisces so this is far away from rationality. Your intuition will be high, you just need to dare to listen.

Thursday 27th

Your home and family are demanding your energy. You need to make sure you stand up for yourself as well as trying to deal with them compassionately. Your parents are trying their best even though it might not look like this to you.

Friday 28th

The first half of today might make you feel a little off, and you might be distracted thinking about what is going on at home and how to sort it out. Later today you will solve the problem and can enjoy your free time, maybe by playing with the kids or letting your inner child out to play.

Saturday 29th

Mercury retrograde is in pleasant conversation with Uranus, and this can lead to unexpected ideas and insights. Don't let yourself be dragged into a power play regarding your home and family life. You can win, but the aim is to create a win-win for both parties, and this cannot be achieved today.

MARCH
. . . .

Sunday 1st
This is very grounding energy, and you could go out for a mountain climb today. You make sure you have enough resources so nothing can get in the way. Connecting to Earth is always something that you appreciate and should do consistently. Make sure your tucker bag is filled with something delicious.

Monday 2nd
What a fantastic start to the week. You roll up your sleeves and just go and get everything done, be it at home, at work or your fitness routine. You check everything off your list and others might wonder how you do it. The only downside is you cannot rest and sit still.

Tuesday 3rd
We are in the imaginative Pisces phase, and whilst you are curious to figure out if there is a way to prove whether things are real, you are also questioning them. What dreams were you thinking about or having in your sleep during the New Moon on February 23rd?

Wednesday 4th

Things can be exciting. Just as you are pondering those dreams, Mercury shifts backwards into Aquarius, which is unusual but here the unexpected is the usual. The Moon is in your house of relationships with Venus on edge in Aries, which could lead to some weird ideas about moving in or out.

Thursday 5th

Venus comes home into Taurus, and there she will brighten your day and bring you some fun, pleasure and joy. She will also help you connect to your beauty, and you will love to surround yourself with beautiful things even more than you usually do. It is an excellent transit to have.

Friday 6th

For a while now we have had these showdowns going down every month between the Moon and Saturn, both in their houses of rulership and in the presence of a lunar node. It creates awareness of your limits and inner restrictions and where you reject love. Focus on receiving and nurturing.

Saturday 7th

You might want to show your best side today especially in a very personal and private way. Express yourself clearly; otherwise there can be misunderstandings as you approach this very differently from the way you usually would, which might lead to confusion. Have pride in yourself.

Sunday 8th

Definitely not the usual Sunday. Venus, ruler of Taurus, is hugging with Uranus to teach you about how to revolutionise self-love and self-expression, while the Sun-Neptune hug makes things blurry. You could feel clear and grounded one minute and floating away the next. Expect the unexpected.

Monday 9th

Powerful Full Moon in Virgo. Neptune is still involved and highlights this energy to the max. You are so torn between the near and the far, but the far seems clearer, more real and manageable. Pretend you can do anything you want to and do it wherever you want to. Where would you go?

Tuesday 10th

Just after you have contemplated yesterday's travel ideas, Mercury is ready to shift gears and move forward again. You did enough research, rethinking and re-evaluating your way to communicate. Coming up next is the integration of your discoveries and a different way to deliver them more compassionately.

Wednesday 11th

During the next two weeks, you might work super hard. Your planetary ruler Saturn is on the final degree in your sign, and this will push you towards completing every task where you have left some loose ends. This is true for all areas, but you won't leave anything to chance.

Thursday 12th

You are searching for connections but most likely for those that will support you and enhance your power in a public role. You could meet important people and connect to new circles. Make sure these circles are indeed worthy of your trust. Do not surround yourself with sycophants.

Friday 13th

It is the perfect day for an after work hang-out with your friends, the real and trustworthy ones. You don't need to do anything fancy, you might just want to sit together, have some good food, share your thoughts and release some of this week's tension.

Saturday 14th

A powerful day to begin with but on a very internal and spiritual level. It is a perfect day to do spiritual work, to meditate, do yoga, go on a retreat etc. Create as much space in your day as you can. If you are not into spirituality, connect to nature and allow your thoughts to flow.

Sunday 15th

The need to draw back and retreat might be even more
significant today. Mercury is on his final day in Aquarius,
and this will have you thinking very logically. In case you
need solutions it is good energy to work with and make
use of. Let your inner genius out.

Monday 16th

Not sure if you like this energy. Mercury is back in
Pisces which makes you more intuitive and irrational,
something you cannot handle well when you want
to finish your projects. Try to use the energy to your
advantage to sense things you usually don't which might
save the day in the end.

Tuesday 17th

Uranus squared the nodes once they entered Capricorn
and Cancer back in the autumn of 2018. Now he makes
an easy connection, so it is likely you will experience this
as a very supportive influence that helps you to follow
the road you have been following in the last 17 months.

Wednesday 18th

The Capricorn party is back, as the Moon meets up
with bigger planets all in your sign. You are likely to be
busy too, and it is possible that your mood shifts quite
quickly. But the force is yours, and you know how to
work hard and be determined.

Thursday 19th

The Moon in Aquarius allows you to mellow. Not that they would call you mellow yellow, but even for you it is good to take a breath and take a break. It is possible that you come up with something that will make your work easier after you have invested some more hours in setting it up.

Friday 20th

Happy Spring Equinox! It is the Sun in Aries time, and so it is time to focus on home, family and ancestors. Mars is hugging Jupiter, and these two combined in your sign are a power pack. Significant expansion ahead. Are you ready for a big deal?

Saturday 21st

You might not be ready for the weekend as your conscientiousness is high, but you still desire to just peace out today. The Moon is joining Mercury in Pisces and it is not the right energy to work on a project. This energy asks you to surrender control and float a little. Just for the weekend.

Sunday 22nd

You cannot steal Sunday and make it a Monday, Capricorn! It is Sunday, and it is a major one you should keep in mind. Saturn, your planetary ruler, leaves your sign and enters Aquarius. This is the beginning of a new era. Do you hear the winds of change?

Monday 23rd

Isn't it amazing how the universe has got your back and is buffering some of this intense energy? Mars is hugging Pluto today, and these two combined are a bomb. It is the soul aligning with its agent of action. Let today's action be guided by intuition to achieve incredible results.

Tuesday 24th

Impossible to take a breath! Happy New Moon in Aries. This is a critical New Moon that might bring up some tension, but this is necessary to transform old, restricting patterns from your childhood. Take good care of your inner child and get ready for a new perception of your youth.

Wednesday 25th

This is the day to catch a breath. So much has been going on during the past days, so try to sort yourself out. Listen to your inner child today and fulfil his or her needs, or temper tantrums could be thrown and you don't want to deal with that energy midweek, do you?

Thursday 26th

Are you ready for the next busy and maybe stressful day? Breathe deep as you can get triggered, especially in the morning. In the afternoon unexpected events might force you to change your plans. A part of you is grateful for the change, as you can escape some family demands.

Friday 27th

At least Friday is smooth and flowing! Honour the day for aligning with your intentions and enjoy the fact that everything you accomplish comes easily today. Treat yourself with some fun and perhaps a meal in company and you could also get yourself something beautiful like a new piece of clothing.

Saturday 28th

Lucky Saturday! Venus and Jupiter in a flowing conversation, expansion and value combined. This could be the day to make a significant investment in something beautiful and worthy, and you could also try your luck with a lottery ticket.

Sunday 29th

Gemini Moon, you swirl around soon. It is Sunday, you could rest but you won't. You swirl around like a buzzing bee and get your home straight, go out jogging, make the breakfast, set up next week's schedule, do the laundry, wash the car, walk the dog and just maybe make it to bed sometime.

Monday 3oth

If you found some sleep, you get up early; if you didn't you are either still up and worked throughout the night or are up early despite all odds. Until noon your energy level is high with Mars on the edge of your sign. Sudden tiredness could arise once he shifts signs.

Tuesday 31st

Mars in Aquarius meets your ruler Saturn on the doorstep. You were all ready to go and change the world, but there might be some restrictions and obligations that could provoke your rebellious side to come out. Don't inflict this on your mate as this energy belongs solely to you.

APRIL

. . . .

Wednesday 1st

Spend some time with your partner and search for the
Emerald City right in your neighbourhood together.
In reality, this could be watching the movie together or
going out to the theatre. Do try and get away from the
usual day to day and sprinkle some magic.

Thursday 2nd

There can be good news today about a gift coming
from your family. It will be something that supports you
and adds to your resources. It could also be something
precious that is given to you in trust, and it is now your
task to keep it.

Friday 3rd

Venus is done with enhancing your self-expression
and moves into Gemini, which for you has a lot to do
with making your everyday life more beautiful. You
will find that your day-to-day will change quite a bit
in the grand scheme, not only through the next three
months but beyond.

Saturday 4th

Just as Venus enters this significant space, she makes a beautiful connection to Saturn, just to make sure everything is on a reliable basis but nevertheless very different from before. It is a perfect day to dream about that new day today. What could it look like? Let your imagination play.

Sunday 5th

Jupiter and Pluto meet for their first of three hugs now. They are very different, but potentially this will combine your highest most optimistic perspective with your deepest desires and shadows. Don't take anything lightly that happens throughout the next few days. You are doing some deep soul work.

Monday 6th

What do you want to educate yourself about, or what beliefs are coming up for you big time? What would you love to transform with the insights you are receiving? Your world might feel a little upside down, but it is good, as change is a universal law,

Tuesday 7th

Previously subconscious thoughts may rise to the surface. You are focused on work and your reputation, and there is a new way to approach things that will help you progress in the long run. You may not know how to really act things out, though, and could be frustrated.

Wednesday 8th

Happy Full Moon in Libra! This is in your area of career and business and could indicate that you receive approval. Mercury connects to Jupiter which can represent an opening of the mind to ideas and thoughts that have been out of your sight and that you did not consider possible before.

Thursday 9th

Instead of sharing secrets with all of your friends, the solution is to share them in a very intimate setting with just the closest and most trustworthy. You can feel triggered today and it might be hard not to react. See if you can leave the situation before acting in a hurtful way.

Friday 10th

Get out your handy dandy notebook and write down what seems to be important in your everyday life, especially things that you feel are not in alignment or do not work out: those where you feel icky but stick to it because it is a habit. You will have the opportunity to make adjustments.

Saturday 11th

You want to have some privacy and spend time in nature. It is a perfect way for you to ease, get grounded and relax. Your mind can be very active now and is much more engaged with forward momentum. Home and family might be something you ponder.

Sunday 12th

What if you had the option to move your home to another place? This might apply in the medium-term, but it might be the first time you play with the idea. It could be about owning a new home, not just renting it. Only allow your thoughts to wander, no decisions need to be made.

Monday 13th

Lots of focus and determination is available to you. It is a fantastic start to the week, and you know your priorities. You could come off a little distant and maybe snippy, but you do not mean to be, it is just you sometimes forget to look left and right if you are absorbed with work.

Tuesday 14th

A feeling of insecurity could rise inside yourself. There is lots of intensity throughout the day. You might find yourself questioning your current situation, especially regarding home and family life. Just observe, the emotional intensity will ease quickly; also the topic itself will stick around a little longer.

Wednesday 15th

Now you are aware that there are some limiting beliefs left regarding your family of origin or even your ancestors, you need to understand them and get a broader perspective. It is challenging to do so. Remember nobody is to blame, as everyone did as best they could.

Thursday 16th

A sense of future is in the air today as the moon is crossing over Mars and is also in flowing conversation with Venus. Do something different today. Eat different food, try a new route to work or home. If you usually watch TV, read a book. Just try and have some variation in your everyday life.

Friday 17th

The weekend is near, and you actually feel like you accomplished a lot this week. With your mind working more forcefully you have proved you have a lot of drive, but somehow you like the intuitive approach. You can try to tune into that to resolve some of the family conflict going on.

Saturday 18th

An idea strikes your mind that would actually improve your home and day-to-day life beautifully. It might take some time to implement it but start to communicate it to your family members right away and see what they have to say. Fingers crossed, they are up for the idea, remain patient if they are not.

Sunday 19th

With the Sun entering your area of self-expression and hobbies you can maintain the balance between work and leisure time. This time can bring more joy into your life. All you need is the will to dedicate some time to fun and the things that make your heart sing.

Monday 20th

You realise how supportive it is to connect to your creative desires and do something that counterbalances the seriousness and responsibility in your life. You might surprise your partner with getting home earlier today to create some time for togetherness. If you feel tired, it is okay to snuggle up.

Tuesday 21st

How does fun and self-expression connect to your values? Do you struggle with taking time off because you feel you need to do something that is useful? Can you even relax? It is possible your hobbies are quite active, but what makes you believe you are not allowed to rest?

Wednesday 22nd

Energy feels very flat today, so it is a weird midweek day. Should a conflict arise within the family, you could react coldly and distantly. Especially if you are confronted with anger. You do not need to be strong all the time. Try and show your vulnerable side.

Thursday 23rd

Happy New Moon in Taurus! You can now literally plant some seeds, especially with regards to finding equilibrium in you work and leisure time. If you want to start a new hobby or intensify the time you dedicate to it, set your intentions and watch them grow.

Friday 24th

You might want to call it a day early and leave all the thoughts regarding work right where they belong - at work. Instead, invest time in your hobby and enhance the fun and joy in your life. You also might want to spend some time with children.

Saturday 25th

Today can be challenging as the events make it crystal clear that change in your own behaviour is inevitable. You can no longer keep the same attitude. The Moon comes into Gemini so you will like to try and avoid the feeling of discomfort by being active all day long.

Sunday 26th

Powerful day, once again! The Sun hugs Uranus, and that just screams at you to expect the unexpected. Your mind is stretched, and with Pluto going retrograde you start to work on change and transformation. Take good care of yourself and start the day grounded and with a good breakfast.

Monday 27th

If you have a chance to be on annual leave this week, you would really enjoy it. You are much more focused on your partner, leisure time and fun in general. It is okay – you deserve it! In case you have to work, it is hopefully at a time where you can fulfil your duties without much effort.

Tuesday 28th

This is the final time the Moon crosses the north node in Cancer. By now you might have realised that there is more to life than work and that especially your relationship and the others in your life play a significant role you should never neglect. It is vital for your life.

Wednesday 29th

With all these changes going on, you feel grateful to receive the nourishment your partner or others provide in your life. It is a perfect day to say thank you, not only to your partner, but also to yourself for continuing and evolving throughout this process. Acknowledge yourself Capricorn!

Thursday 30th

Money might be a thing coming to your mind these days. Do you have enough resources, and how are you handling them? What about the resources you share with others? You might consider working less and instead increase your leisure time. It can be a great day to calculate your money.

MAY

. . . .

Friday 1st

Keep your notebook handy as you might have a sudden idea sometime today or tomorrow so just write down what comes to mind. You might need to find a sense of balance between what is yours and what you share, so maybe it is an excellent day to buy a present for yourself or somebody close to you.

Saturday 2nd

You like the Moon in Virgo as it enhances your sense of practicality and allows you to make thorough plans. This is one of your secrets to leading your projects to success. Currently, you might want to plan and envision how you want to organise your spare time and your hobbies.

Sunday 3rd

It is a beautiful and flowing Sunday open for your exploration. Nothing forceful or challenging so you can recharge your batteries. You could want to plan the next vacation or consider a new topic to study and broaden your horizon. Whatever you choose it will help you to progress further.

Monday 4th

Ready for the beginning of the week you want to focus on your career and reputation. Mercury hugs the Sun today so there might be some more insights waiting for you regarding your hobbies, creativity or children. It can take a while before you get the message, so to speak. Let it sink in.

Tuesday 5th

The nodes have been in your area of self and other for a while, and you worked on a lot on these themes. Today they shift to your area of day to day life as well as your inner reflection and spiritual connection. It is a critical time that will improve your everyday life.

Wednesday 6th

Time to see some friends! It is just midweek, but you do feel the need to connect and get out. Call up your friends and have a fun afternoon tea, or an evening out. While you share what has happened in each other's lives one or two secrets might be revealed.

Thursday 7th

Happy Full Moon in Scorpio! This highlights your friendships and social circles, and you can gratefully have a look around at what people make up your inner circle. Those are the ones who are genuinely supportive of you and don't hesitate to tell you the truth. Cheers to all of them!

Friday 8th

It is the end of the week, and you start to seek a little rest and retreat. It is the first time that the Moon has crossed the south node so you might have to ask yourself, do you hold religious or spiritual beliefs that limit you? Is the belief system you held ten years ago still valid?

Saturday 9th

You feel a sense of power today, and it can quickly happen that you somehow are set in charge during one of your hobbies. Nothing can hide your leadership skills, not even in your free time. Before you say yes, ask yourself how much responsibility you want to take on if any at all.

Sunday 10th

You might think about what can bring you more joy and allow yourself to be very optimistic. Or you should at least try optimism. How does it feel for you to see opportunities and possibilities in the broader scope? A Capricorn can make almost everything possible.

Monday 11th

Your planetary ruler Saturn has now tested the Aquarian water and decides to go back home. To anchor in the new, there have to be some finishing touches to the old, and you want to set everything straight before you move on. The foundation has to be stable.

Tuesday 12th

Today your heart and mind are in a great conversation and investigating your future. What does it need to feel like, what about day to day life and what sense of self-worth is necessary to get there? You will be busy today so roll up your sleeves and go.

Wednesday 13th

It is likely that today or in the last few days, something happens that will remain a theme in your life throughout the next three months. It probably has something to do with your everyday life, your daily routine, health or work. Venus is retrograde, and the theme is revealed.

Thursday 14th

Mars has made its way to Pisces. Not a place he likes to be, as it buffers his sense of action. Think running under water, and you get the idea. It allows you a state of more calmness and surrender, instead of go, go, go, being busy all the time.

Friday 15th

Jupiter starts to move retrograde so, for now, you have reached the maximum expansion and can now think about what boundaries you might need to keep or what needs to change to bring more optimism in. It is a great day to go to the cinema or read a book.

Saturday 16th

What things from your present existence do you want to have in your future life? This is a question you might ponder today. It is an issue of getting out of your comfort zone. Are you willing to leave yours, and what could be left behind?

Sunday 17th

This Sunday is about family and roots. It is also about children, playtime and maybe you are about to take on a new role in your life. Aunt, uncle, mum, dad, granny or granddad. The energy is bright and lively, and it is quite a day to enjoy.

Monday 18th

Your emotions are in a natural connection with your mind. You feel really powerful and alive. Don't let your mind run around in circles instead make sure to you express your ideas through talking or writing. Your telephone might ring a lot today.

Tuesday 19th

Consider the role of your home in your everyday life. What could make your home more beautiful or what could make your day-to-day life more comfortable and graceful? You feel good today, and that is because you know your roots sustain you, so there is the space to let true beauty emerge.

Wednesday 20th

We have a double shift happening today. First the Moon enters your area of self-expression, and later the Sun leaves that space and enters Gemini, and with that joins the north node and Venus. So from the start, the universe is boosting your evolution to where you go, because you already resolved so much.

Thursday 21st

You could feel a little tired and like you cannot keep up with the pace that the energy is asking for. The Sun in Gemini is really active and not resting, while the Moon in Taurus seeks comfort pleasure and chill time. Be compassionate with yourself and allow yourself some rest.

Friday 22nd

Happy New Moon in Gemini! This is a fresh spark of energy, and you are once again asked to set a goal. This New Moon is particularly crucial as it sets the tone for the next 18 months instead of only six months. What is the highest image and version of your everyday life?

Saturday 23rd

The shift and changing of emotions that you feel with
the Moon in Gemini is in conflict with your currently
muffled energetic expression of Mars in Pisces.
Fundamentally Mars in Pisces asks you to surrender,
and that is something you do have a massive problem
with. Surrender is releasing control, and that doesn't
come easily to you.

Sunday 24th

This is the first imprint the Moon leaves on its new
north node, and with this New Moon you set out to find
the first things on your list for achieving a new improved
everyday life. Start with writing your list: definitely get it
out on paper, it cannot solely live in your mind.

Monday 25th

This Monday you want to create some space to hook up
with your partner. You will nurture them and be more open
to just cuddling and hanging out than you usually are.
Thanks to the connection of Moon and Mars you do want
to surrender and that might be better behind closed doors

Tuesday 26th

As there was flow yesterday, today there is tension. Pluto in opposition to the Moon is always a little challenging because your sense of security and nurturing in your partnership can feel threatened. The Moon moves fast though, so this passes. Don't make a mountain out of a molehill.

Wednesday 27th

Today it is possible to hear you roar, especially if you feel like you are intimidated. You seem to have an aura of authority all around you, but when it comes to showing your deep inner stuff you generally believe that attack is the best form of defence. It is a mask, but a proven one.

Thursday 28th

Mercury is wearing his seven-league boots and has rushed through his own sign. He is now moving into Cancer where he will take a more extended rest. So relationships are back in focus big time, in a different way than before but not less important.

Friday 29th

The Virgo Moon is challenging and supportive for all this Gemini energy. You get a good sense of practicality or realism, checking stuff off and making plans. On the other hand, this carries you outside of the usual day-to-day as it has you thinking about travel and exploration.

Saturday 30th

The tension between everyday life and your sense of adventure might be fruitful as the catalyst that allows your mind and spirit to see a new version of your everyday life. Your thoughts need to drift away to anchor in what is original. There is no need for restrictions as of yet.

Sunday 31st

Enjoy the morning energy, flip through a travel brochure and allow your mind and feelings to go to utopia. Once the afternoon comes, you might already be focused on Monday and the start of work again. Allow your mind to wander as long as you can.

JUNE
....

Monday 1st
At the beginning of this week, you find new ways
to approach your work. Your sense of practicality
and structure, as well as the busy bee aspect the
Sun brings in from Gemini, support you in getting
a lot done and impressing some of your co-workers.
Acknowledge your progress!

Tuesday 2nd
Mars uncomfortably nudges Venus. Someone in your
immediate environment might blurt out something that
you have been trying to overlook for a while. You might
want to act on it, but you cannot yet. Just throw them a
nasty look, for now. You have to figure out the problem.

Wednesday 3rd
Venus *Cazimi* time. That means Venus hugs the Sun
and metamorphoses from evening star to morning
star. She enters an entirely new space and time of
existence. It is a sign that the shifts you are about to
make in your everyday life will give you more strength,
beauty and brightness.

Thursday 4th

Significant tension today, as again you would love to dream for your future. You still feel sensitive, as well as not really wanting to deal with people. Everybody had better stay away. The release point for this is to let your mind wander back to utopia, considering how to make it real.

Friday 5th

Happy Full Moon in Sagittarius! Did anybody ask for more tension? This Full Moon is focusing on your beliefs and also on your spiritual values. Carefully observe your opinions and let the ones go that are no longer serving you, even if they did in the past. Leave no stone unturned.

Saturday 6th

Dream a little dream of me. You want to retreat from the world and dwell in fantasies or meditation. Make sure you do not lose your grounding. The energy is a little too fast and fluctuating for you, so retreating into nature is a sure way to remain grounded to mother earth.

Sunday 7th

Thankfully the Moon comes into your sign, and this brings in a more serious tone as well as having a grounding effect on you. If there is anything to do today, you will be in the perfect mood to get all the things done that usually get left till last.

Monday 8th

The Moon is in Capricorn without the south node or Saturn and with nothing significant in opposition, so it is a relief. You are able to gather your strength and focus, just have a smooth running day, even though or maybe because it is a busy one.

Tuesday 9th

Another natural and flowing day for you. Two quiet days in a row seems unbelievable! While you are in your element, beware not to fall into old traps of being too strict or rigid. You are goal oriented and determined but by now might have learned to look left and right, to see if others can keep up.

Wednesday 10th

Take everything that happens today with a pinch of salt. Falling for an illusion is easy. If something looks too good to be true it probably is. The opposite could also happen today: a significant disillusionment is unveiled, presenting you with the pure raw truth.

Thursday 11th

A very realistic approach is still needed to cope with the energy throughout the next three days as the Moon is enhancing the power of illusions. It is likely that this energy plays out in your neighbourhood or with your siblings and that it will affect your everyday life.

Friday 12th

A sense of magic and imagination is in the air as you are trying hard to find beauty in your life. You would love to integrate more of your core values and live a more authentic experience, and that is what you are actually called to do. What has to shift for that to happen?

Saturday 13th

It is a very confusing day. The Moon as well as Mars both hug Neptune today. While these three hang out together, it is a good idea to go swimming and connect to water. Take the day off if you can. No serious rational action: instead retreat and dream away.

Sunday 14th

Imagine where your actions can take you. That is the underlying theme. Mars is slowly moving away from Neptune so you might not feel as unclear as you did before and yet it is not the right time to act. Your feelings could give you a hint of where future roads might lead to.

Monday 15th

Heart and mind are in a discussion, and it is likely that the heart will win this time. Seriously, listen to your heart! What is it whispering to your ears about your home and your roots, your sense of emotional safety? How do you need to be nurtured?

Tuesday 16th

This is a fun and stabilising day, as the Moon connects to the Sun and later ingresses Taurus. Grounding and a good sense of pleasure arises, and you want to indulge in the beauty and cornucopia of life. Laugh, dance, have a barbecue with just the best food you can find.

Wednesday 17th

Possibly you had a short night as you were up celebrating or you slept fitfully. It might need a stronger breakfast tea than usual, but once you are awake, it is an easy day. Thankfully there are no significant events nor challenges, and you might even be able to have more leisure time than expected.

Thursday 18th

Your latest insights regarding safety, nourishment and relationships bring up the need to rethink, re-evaluate and reconsider your perspective and approach during the next three weeks while Mercury is retrograde in Cancer. It is a time to focus and observe your feelings and emotional reactions and value them.

Friday 19th

A sense of joy is rising in you as you are fully engaged with your life. You feel precisely where things are heading and at least inside of yourself make a commitment to act accordingly. It can be a fated day, the universe is sending you signs and is showing you the way.

Saturday 20th

Mars and Jupiter's connections are a powerhouse of
energy as Jupiter can enhance the power available to
Mars. So it is possible that you feel a boost of energy like
a million dollars. Just spend the day the way you want
to, enjoy the buoyancy and have a wonderful solstice
celebration.

Sunday 21st

The Sun is at its peak, the day is as long as it can be
and then you have the New Moon solar eclipse just
on the doorstep. That means new starts for healthy
relationships, a new way of coping with your feelings, a
need and urgency to prioritise emotions.

Monday 22nd

Whoever you meet and interact with today, let your
emotions guide you. Trust your gut and make your
decisions in a way that serves the people and not just
the system. Utility and productivity are fine, but the key
is to use the system to help humankind.

Tuesday 23rd

Get your dream journal ready. Neptune is moving retrograde, and this can play out either with an enhancement of your dreams, or the opposite: a decrease in your ability to remember your dreams. At least during this shift, there are often messages rising from the subconscious and appearing in dreams.

Wednesday 24th

Today is more chilled, as there is not much happening astrologically speaking. With the Moon in Leo, you might want to think about where you want to be or how to use your resources to use your presence in the world. You need to be all in, because Leo energy is very personal to you.

Thursday 25th

Venus moves direct today! She has now transformed herself to a bright and beautiful morning star, and you can spot her if you get up early in the morning as she rises before the Sun. You feel more strength and your ability to shine in your everyday life can no longer be dismissed.

Friday 26th

The energy feels much more intense by the end of this week. Mars is squaring the nodes as you try to figure out the right way to act to get from where you are, to where you want to go. Strange feelings from the past could come to the surface. You are asked to respond differently.

Saturday 27th

Mars is on its final day in Pisces, and it brings up sensitivities and old wounds big time. Do you want to feel sorry for yourself and focus on despair or do you want to leave the past behind? You cannot change what has happened, but you can take the lesson learned and move on.

Sunday 28th

Happy Sunday and welcome to Mars in Aries, his sign of rulership. For you this concerns family, ancestors, roots, home and your family life. It is a place where you learn to assert yourself and you have plenty of time for the lesson as Mars will stay here for the remainder of this year.

Monday 29th

Monday is a busy and probably stressful day as the
Moon is in dispute with Jupiter, Pluto and Saturn. So
your mood can shift and change several times, and you
are asked to keep calm and stay true to yourself. It can
be a challenge because you want to please and fulfil the
expectations of others.

Tuesday 30th

You are invited to go deep today. Emotionally and also
regarding your beliefs. Jupiter and Pluto approach
their second hug. Can you acknowledge all parts from
yourself when you approach them from a more emotional
perspective? How do you feel with regards to your
shadow? Some strength might wait to come to light.

JULY

. . . .

Wednesday 1st

Mercury is in the arms of the Sun, and you are about
to understand some of your deeper emotional needs
and why you want to be nurtured in a certain way. This
might also apply to some of the roles you take on in
your relationships.

Thursday 2nd

Saturn returns to Capricorn to check if everything is in
order. You get another chance to lay the right structure
to execute your life effectively. You get almost six more
months with Saturn, so use this time wisely. Your hard
work will pay off.

Friday 3rd

When was the last time you spent solely with yourself?
This is a broad hint to do so. You might also want
to engage in your spiritual work such as doing
yoga, meditating or just connecting to nature itself.
Everything that has a soothing effect and connects you
to your inside is highlighted.

Saturday 4th

The weekend is here, and you could feel an imbalance
between your plans and your partner's demands.
Try to compromise in a way that creates a win-win
situation for both of you. So neither of you needs to
end up with a grumpy face or does anything for the
sake of peace and quiet.

Sunday 5th

Happy Full Moon in Capricorn. This is your Full
Moon. What did you ponder around Boxing Day 2019
that is now ready to harvest? You went through lots
of changes regarding your mask, persona and your
individuality. Acknowledge how far you have come
and who you are right now.

Monday 6th

Currently, a lot of energy is focusing on emotions, and
it is possible you choose to disconnect today. This can
irritate your partner, especially if you fail to communicate
with them. Let them know it is nothing personal and you
need a moment to adjust. Try some handicraft activities.

Tuesday 7th

You might want to check on your bank account and
savings. For all your future plans it is vital you know
which resources are available and where you are aiming
for. Cash up and if there is more than you expected you
might spare a little and get a treat for your honey.

Wednesday 8th

Mars in Aries is impatient, pushing and wants everything immediately and sometimes at any cost. This is in conflict with your mind trying to consider all of the emotions, feelings and needs. You can feel frustrated, but some physical activity will help you to find ease and release tension.

Thursday 9th

You could feel as if you are walking into the wind as your surroundings have not yet adjusted to your new approach to your health and daily life. The vision you created in your mind is not fully integrated into your life. Pull up your strength to stand firm against that wind. Nobody shall dampen your light!

Friday 10th

What about a magical Friday? This is a day that asks you to sprinkle some fairy dust on your interactions with your significant other, a friend or a business partner. Some people might think you are not into this sort of thing and could be surprised. From time to time you have no objections to magic.

Saturday 11th

The Moon is coming into Aries, so it is probably a day to interact with family or start to move things around in your home. It is in no way a restful Saturday, as the Moon is also crossing Mars. Be cautious, you might lose your temper, and you know family triggers are the most effective of all.

Sunday 12th

Have a happy sunny Sunday! Mercury is finally moving direct, and you might have discovered what nurturing means to you, how you want to nurtured and how you want to be nurtured. You will still be feeling your way through for a little longer, but the hardest part of the ride is done!

Monday 13th

A little more tension might be present today. You feel that something has to change in your home or family life to make this new start in your personal relationships a success. Success means fulfilment, the unhindered flow of love and nourishment. Observe today's events, do not react.

Tuesday 14th

It is likely to be an exciting day. Sun with Jupiter days are most often beneficial even if they connect through an opposition. You are asked to find equilibrium between your needs and the demands of others in your life. There might be a surprise around the corner, and it might be a luscious one.

Wednesday 15th

It is a Sun-Pluto day and much more intense than yesterday. No surprises, but you are searching for comfort while things are falling apart. Most likely, a way you have seen yourself or the way you have been perceived is shifting. It is shifting to allow a more authentic version of you to shine through.

Thursday 16th

The energy is easing now. You can expect the day to be busy and fly by, with you being involved in work and your new routines. Your mind might be very active wanting to understand all these emotional things logically, but you cannot rationalise emotion. You have to feel it.

Friday 17th

The Moon meets Venus Morningstar, and you might be able to spot both of them in the morning sky. Bright and beautiful, they invite you to connect and be curious. Ask many questions throughout your day and don't forget to listen to the answer you receive before you investigate further.

Saturday 18th

The Moon is coming back to its favourite place in Cancer, and once again you like to focus on your partnership. It is an excellent opportunity to spend this weekend in intimate togetherness. This can be at home or on a trip, but it is likely not too far from home.

Sunday 19th

Your mind and emotion are in alignment today. This helps you express your true feelings and is almost calling for an oath of love or some poetry. Loving messages are a thing, and this could also be about hiding love notes all over your home to have them discovered whenever it is time.

Monday 20th

Happy New Moon in Cancer, again! Yes, second-chance New Moon, now that the retrograde is completed and Venus is direct you have a much clearer understanding of your needs and how true comfort feels for you. Saturn is asking for commitment, and a marriage proposal is a possibility.

Tuesday 21st

The Moon is trying out Leo's fire ahead of the Sun. If everything has gone to plan, you are now high on love, with yourself and your partner. Don't underestimate self-love – it is the vital part and key to every successful relationship. When you love yourself, your cup is full.

Wednesday 22nd

The Sun is entering Leo, and for the next thirty days you can increase your self-love, the intimacy in your partnership and have a good look at all the resources in your life. Pay particular attention to everything related to family and home, there might be something cooking.

Thursday 23rd

It's been a while since you focused on travelling. In case you want to plan a long distance journey, this is a great time to move forward with it in regards to all the nitty-gritty details. You probably dislike leaving anything to a chance. Get the checklist written or tick it off.

Friday 24th

A dream vs reality day. What is real and what is not? What lies beyond your imagination and what does not? Do you dare to step out of your comfort zone, or don't you? You might feel the urge to pinch yourself if something happens that you thought beyond the range of possibilities.

Saturday 25th

This weekend you think a lot about your public image and reputation. Maybe there is an event you need to attend to represent your company or even yourself. As long as you show up for something you are wholeheartedly connected to, nothing can go wrong.

Sunday 26th

Wherever you attend, make sure you take your partner with you. Otherwise, there could be conflict as your partner might feel like you want to hide them or only care about the audience but not about them. As this is not true, try to prevent it right away.

Monday 27th

You need somebody to talk to, but which of your friends is the one to keep the secret? There could be disillusionment regarding your neighbourhood, which leads to consequences in your everyday life and tension about your home with your partner. Lots to handle. Try to stay calm.

Tuesday 28th

Neptune connects to his brother Jupiter, the co-ruler of Pisces. This means you consider ever broadening perspectives and have the ability for boundless imagination. Beware not to float away, but it is a good time to connect to the universe, your spirit guides and god.

Wednesday 29th

Time for a happy dance, while Venus is leaving her shadow phase today. The retrograde is over, the results of this are crystal clear and you are now able to make progress. So maybe it will soon be time for decisions or adding more to the changes you have already made.

Thursday 30th

Another fantastic day for meditation, spiritual work, retreat and beautiful insights. You might intuitively know something, or your feelings could guide you to have an experience or even make a decision. Signs could come up in your dreams. If you can, spend the day near water, at the beach or a pool.

Friday 31st

The Moon is coming back to your sign, and this brings a serious tone to Friday, or let's say a stabilising one. It might be necessary to take some work home with you, or you might feel like you need to rework something because you had some breaks during the week.

AUGUST
. . . .

Saturday 1st
Something unconscious can become conscious. In this lies tremendous power. The awareness of a shadow, trigger or habit can help you to change your behaviour and eventually to heal and transform an issue. This is most likely linked to your ability to receive nurturing and caring.

Sunday 2nd
The universe might have a surprise in store, so expect the unexpected. Does it bring pleasure or disruption? It can go either way, but actually, the chances are higher that it turns out in your favour. Its purpose is to act as a wake-up call you cannot ignore.

Monday 3rd
Happy Full Moon in Aquarius. This is an excellent time to have a hard look at your possessions, and decide which of them are of actual value. Unloved gifts, junk, and unused items take up space. You have to create space for the new to come, so go and declutter like there's no tomorrow.

Tuesday 4th

Mars is in discussion with Jupiter. It is about beliefs, hopes, optimism and the need to stand up for yourself and have the courage to be yourself amongst your family. Temper triggers abound, and you could be tempted to throw tantrums.

Wednesday 5th

The Moon in Pisces helps to ease the energy significantly. Mercury moves into Leo, so you have completed another lesson in understanding how to relate, nurture and receive. The next lesson is understanding your resources and how to take part without overpowering others. Are you ready to shed more light on that topic?

Thursday 6th

Venus has made it to the north node, and you have already made some significant advancement in beautifying your everyday life. This connection might put the cherry on the cake. Pay attention to the signs and synchronicities today, there are no coincidences. There are hints where your path is leading you.

Friday 7th

Venus is now moving in your area of relationships. Now that you have mental clarity and understanding, Venus will help you to apply everything you learned. Be fair, allow equality, and a real balance of giving and receiving. The receiving part might be the hardest for you. Just do your best.

Saturday 8th

You can feel angry or pushy today, impulsive and impatient at least. You might be surprised how people perceive you in this condition because you can be kind of rough. A 'my way or the highway' attitude won't get you far. Open yourself to the possibility that there is no need to fight.

Sunday 9th

There is no need to defend either. In case conflict with family arises just try the approach that they do not mean to diminish you or your opinion. Agree to disagree and see how much peace that can create. You can stick with your truth and allow another view. Amazing right?

Monday 10th

The Moon in Taurus brings beautiful energy for you. It makes an excellent connection to Venus, so it is an excellent day for love, pleasure and beauty. There will probably be a soft and warm tone to this day, and if you can get some delicious food involved, it might feel like heaven. Happy surprises are possible.

Tuesday 11th

Mind games could happen, as you try to align your feeling and thoughts. Perception is key to your experience and to change that perspective might be a hard thing to do right now. There is a tendency to be stubborn and not move an inch. Ground and breathe deeply to feel better.

Wednesday 12th

There is a sense of restlessness, and there will be lots of questions coming up for you, but you can cope with that energy by filling your day with various activities. This is a great opportunity to get some things done that you have procrastinated about, as long as they are tasks that need short-term focus.

Thursday 13th

Power struggle. Today you want to know who is in charge, who is right and who will show their true colours. Create a physical outlet for this energy through activities like sport, running, or doing some challenging physical work in your home. You might be surprised how well you can handle the tension.

Friday 14th

Destruction is a vital part of life. Once again you need to create some space. The tower has to fall to build the new kingdom. What structures in a metaphorical and literal sense need to fall by the wayside regarding your home and family life?

Saturday 15th

This could be such a warm, tender and overall beautiful Saturday that you do not want to waste it on completing everyday tasks. It is a day for love and romance, in a nurturing and a sensual physical way. You could decide to spend the day in bed, and not because you feel tired…

Sunday 16th

Uranus and liberation are deeply connected. When Uranus starts its retrograde motion, it is to free you from restrictions, and that goes double when Uranus is in Taurus. You have not yet tapped into your full potential. The retrograde will leave behind what is holding you back so you can express yourself on a grander scale.

Monday 17th

It is another time for intimacy, authenticity and to tame your ego with the Moon entering into Leo. Energy is falling a little flat which might be a good thing as it minimises your tendency to inflate your ego. Don't take yourself too seriously or believe for a second that you know the truth.

. . . .

Tuesday 18th

Happy New Moon in Leo! Set your goals about being humble and just be yourself without drama and show. The real, authentic you is more than enough, and it is the greatest gift of trust to allow others to see your vulnerability. Resources are available even if you don't behave like a king or queen.

Wednesday 19th

The spirit of adventure is in the air, and the Sun is connecting to the point of past and future developments. You can find that you do want to engage more in life and retreat less or find a way to integrate your spiritual habits into a practical daily routine.

Thursday 20th

The monthly dream vs reality theme is back and with it the see-saw between the travel bug and the comfort zone. The emphasis on wanderlust and thoughtful exploration is stronger than usual. It is also a great time to pick a new study topic and let the mind travel vastly.

Friday 21st

Mental exploration has rarely been more accessible, you can grasp on teachings that you would usually consider too complicated. Make an effort and time to dig in while Mercury is in this area and you will set the foundation to continue your studies successfully.

Saturday 22nd

And as if the Sun knew you could use support she is
entering Virgo, too. Exploration is the keyword for the
next thirty days, and this is mental as well as real-
world explorations. It has to be practical, it has to be
perfect and planned accordingly. A perfect time to
plan a trip from A to Z.

Sunday 23rd

You can get by with a little help from your friends, and
the Scorpio Moon opens you to connect to your friends
and social tribe. You want to meet up with those that can
support your adventure plans, or that would ask you the
right questions to dive deeper into your studies.

Monday 24th

It is like a cosmic stop sign is flaring up. This stop
sign is called Saturn, and he red-cards your aggressive
assertiveness with regards to home and family. He asks
you to focus on respect and temperance. Sport is vital,
the energy has to find an outlet or it can lead to
being accident prone.

Tuesday 25th

Exciting day, some insights and revelations are ahead.
Venus is trying to find balance with Jupiter, but these
two always act for a more significant cause so you
will see that sense of expanded positivity and love for
yourself and others. The key is to search inside yourself
first and foremost.

99

Wednesday 26th

Take some time off and retreat. Listen to your inner voice. There is a lot to tune into. Go out in nature as this connects you to the universal truths and allows you to find what you want to aim for. You might want to go on a hike to add a sense of adventure to your inner exploration.

Thursday 27th

Imagine you are free of limiting beliefs. Fully trust in natural law and stop thinking you know the truth. Instead, you are curious, seeking and open-minded for boundless possibilities. For love and compassion for everyone. Imagine just for a day sitting on the mountaintop is as good as climbing up there.

Friday 28th

Revolution can liberate you from a feeling of being stuck in the mud. You chained yourself to a false sense of security, and with this, you limited your range of self expression. Cut yourself loose, step out of the inner restrictions and strive for maximum uniqueness.

Saturday 29th

There is a lot of nourishing and sustaining Water and Earth energy. Actually quite a mixture, so you will not fly high all day. And yet these days are intense and speak of more profound truth. Be as open-minded as you can be, forget perfectionism, follow the urge to expand without overdoing it.

Sunday 30th

Luckily the Moon is in Aquarius today, so you are
emotionally a little detached; otherwise this heightened
love vibe could be overwhelming. It is as if you
understand in your core essence the principle of
love. Not just earthly love, but divine and impersonal,
collective love. It is intense. Connect and ground
through your breath.

Monday 31st

It is a relatively quiet day: great to rest and to enjoy
the mundane life. When you go shopping, you can be
attracted to something that is usually not your style, but
the energy invites you to experiment, explore and feel
joy. Dance in your garden, have afternoon tea at noon or
take a different route to work.

SEPTEMBER

....

Tuesday 1st

The vision of your future is getting more concrete in front of your very eyes. Once again the balance between the comforting old and the exciting new is highlighted, and yet the emphasis is more on the adventurous side. You realise this is the call you have to make.

Wednesday 2nd

Happy Full Moon in Pisces! The planet of love is in dispute with the planet of business. You might face a real choice today. Will you choose law, principle and efficiency or will you go with love, mercy and kindness? Compassion is high so unveil your gentle attitude.

Thursday 3rd

'If that's what it takes, that's what I do' is an appropriate motto. You have your future vision in mind and the building blocks to make it happen, while you are eager to unleash your moxie. Lots of energy is available to you and there is no need to beat about the bush.

Friday 4th

Your inner yin and yang, your receptive and your forceful sides, are in conflict. Your rational mind is more getting the yin part while your emotions are fiery and impatient and more on the yang part. It is an exciting setup, asking for a creative solution.

Saturday 5th

Mercury had a short stay in Virgo and is already coming into Libra and your area of career and public image. The next three weeks will have your mind walking a tightrope to figure out the approach that serves you best. The key is to weigh your needs and wants enough.

Sunday 6th

What an amazing Sunday! You feel the urge to express yourself freely and artistically and you might have a chance to do it in public! The next weeks enhance your desire to be seen and be perceived as a queen or king. You can create your stage today.

Monday 7th

The morning heralds an unexpected turn of events while the late evening is likely to feel gregarious and joyful. No matter if you are sitting in an open-air pub or in your homelike garden, the talk will delight you and the glasses will chink. Cheers to life!

Tuesday 8th

A day of stabilisation and down-to-earth energy is awaiting you. You are in such a flow that you could dance and you feel like a million dollars. While you perform like a locomotive, there is still a sense of joy and good vibration. Treat yourself once work is done and have some space for fun.

Wednesday 9th

It's Sun–Jupiter day, and those are simply the best. Jupiter is not mainly your guy, but he invites you to be generous and joyous. Why not surprise your loved one with a generous gift, it does not need to be expensive but rather show your big heart. It is there so let it show.

Thursday 10th

Mars retrograde time! This one might be a little tough. Mars in his home sign is super strong and needing to move backwards, setting teeth on edge. You need to take part in sports and physical activity for the time being, otherwise the energy can lead to conflict especially with your family.

Friday 11th

What is real and what is not? The dream vs reality battle is on big time, as it involves the Sun on the weighing scale. With the Moon in your relationship sector, it might be a good call to take off the rose-coloured glasses and face the naked truth. Disillusionment is a bitter but necessary pill to swallow.

Saturday 12th

You stay focused on relationships, but now the important part is to throw your needs into consideration. Your mind wants fairness, justice and true equality. Sudden emotions can surface, and the best thing you can do is to just feel them instead of repressing. Feel deep, feel everything.

Sunday 13th

Jupiter heads direct! Enough of the re-doing, and re-everything at least for Jupiter. It actually makes him quite happy as it means he is on his way out of Capricorn. So you might feel a sense of optimism rising from within just to know that the future has come into reach.

Monday 14th

A powerful and positive transformation. This is the energy that comes of looking at the destroyed tower and knowing it was right to knock it down, as it freed you. It is a lovely morning for togetherness so you might want to get to work a little later.

Tuesday 15th

Today is more of a mixed bag. You could be involved in some kind of drama-queen moment that might make you contemplate your beliefs. Ask all the questions that come to mind and feel the ease once the Moon moves into real and stable earth, and you can determine what your truth is.

Wednesday 16th

Life might feel very real, and it is easy to get caught up in perfectionism especially regarding your career or your public image. Nobody will turn a blind eye to anything so the day can be very strenuous. If you have routine jobs to do the timing is perfect.

Thursday 17th

Happy New Moon in Virgo! This New Moon has a very down to earth attitude, with the Sun and Moon in trine to Saturn, setting the right foundation. You will be creating the perfect, detailed plan for how to construct after all this deconstruction. From here onwards things will soon move ahead.

Friday 18th

Saturn is the bringer of rewards, if you did the work. You surely did the job Capricorn so take a look around at what you are rewarded with. Are you satisfied or is a voice inside you screaming for more? Practise gratitude, the actual key for abundance.

Saturday 19th

You can feel conflicted by the demands of the world, your family and your own needs and desires. How can you reconcile these or act, and why is there still more work to do when you are already giving everything you've got? Don't allow frustration to get the best of you. Go out tonight.

Sunday 20th

You might be out to get Sunday groceries when you suddenly run into a friend you haven't seen in a while. Those unexpected events can light you up like a Christmas tree if you make use of the unexpected opportunity. Enjoy yourself. Happy connecting!

Monday 21st

Schedule your meeting for today, as people will likely be very fruitful and you are in the perfect mood to connect and listen to everybody – which is not always the case. Something said will ask you to stretch your mind, and you should say double thanks to the person coming up with that idea.

Tuesday 22nd

This is interesting energy as one part of you wants to draw back and get some time out of the public eye while another part votes for the opposite. Maybe instead of climbing up your mountain and sitting there hermit style, try to discuss the issues you ponder and open up for new insights.

Wednesday 23rd

There is something you still don't get regarding the desire to please and also with being self-sufficient and following your own rules. As long as you value others' opinions more than your own, this problem will endure. It's hard to win and compromise at the same time.

Thursday 24th

Once again you are called to consider your needs in order to decipher what to act upon. You want to balance on too many levels. What actions do you need to take to install fairness and equality in your home environment? What do you even need to undo?

Friday 25th

With the Moon in your sign and the Sun in your career sector, you make many things happen. First you want to expand the project and get more results, then you need to change the approach and in the end, cut away the excess to receive a practical and reliable product.

Saturday 26th

What about your self-worth Capricorn? Do you honour yourself enough or do you thrive on outside appreciation? Do you receive enough recognition and if not is it possible you are hiding? Allow your unique personality to shine through, and it will be impossible to ignore you.

Sunday 27th

It's good that Mercury now moves into your area of friends and social circles. The Sun is still involved with matters of career and vocation but your mind is about to ponder the trustworthiness of friends. In a discussion you might ask yourself if you are safe in all of your circles.

Monday 28th

It would be magnificent if you could feel as safe to express yourself in your everyday life as you do when engaging with your inner world. There is a good chance you do so today by being interested and curious to learn more. Nobody expects you to know it all. Nobody but you.

Tuesday 29th

Mark the day with a big exclamation mark! Your planetary ruler Saturn is done with moving backwards to test the foundation. From this point onwards the future is irresistible. First, you need to put some finishing touches on everything but get used to the idea of a whole different world.

Wednesday 30th

One of your finishing touches is to get some family stuff straight. This could be about conflicts with some elders or about moving your home to another place. This can be a stressful situation, but you have to make a choice, and you know you are good on that!

OCTOBER

....

Thursday 1st
October kicks off with the Full Moon in Aries. This places everything relating to home and family in the spotlight. It is an area that has been highlighted for some time since Mars entered and it will be for the remainder of 2020. What is your inner child wanting you to see?

Friday 2nd
Venus comes into Virgo. She does not really like to be here, as everything has to be too perfect and too real, but as the ruler of Taurus she is familiar with the Earth element and can support your energy a lot. So if you want to add a sense of value and beauty to your visions, this is a great time to do it!

Saturday 3rd
Here comes the happy Earth trine energy – Moon in Taurus connects to Venus, and they are sending good vibes to you. You feel a wonderful sense of stability and can have lots of fun letting your creativity play. The energy is also breathing life into your travel plans.

Sunday 4th

There is still lots of flow but a sudden question can arise regarding what is yours and what belongs to others. While engaging in a group setting are you still following your own ideas or is there a lemming effect? Make sure you access all of your inner resources, you have plenty.

Monday 5th

While you tap into your creative potential, Pluto the great transformer and destroyer has done enough deconditioning for now and moves direct again. This marks the beginning of a powerful time in which you select what bits and pieces can be reintegrated and which ones are gone for good.

Tuesday 6th

"Sometimes, all I need is the air that I breathe ..." Do you know that song? The lyrics could apply today as the Moon in Gemini flows with the Sun in Libra. You are in a busy, getting things done mode. If you choose challenging tasks, you will have time and energy to get them done.

Wednesday 7th

Keep your ears fully open today. From somewhere there is a piece of information coming in that can totally alter your perspective. This can happen in every situation just while you walk by others, stand in line at the counter or cross the street. Pay particular attention to what friends have to say.

Thursday 8th

It is likely to be another productive day where you check off your to-do list like a pro. Once it's home time, your mood shifts and you are happy to sink into the nurturing arms of your partner. The checklist is forgotten, and you enjoy revelling in togetherness.

Friday 9th

There is still lots of love in the air and no matter how long you have been with your partner or whether or not you are married, you might want to plan a honeymoon! Maybe it is the desire to just get away for a while, at least for a moment?

Saturday 10th

Spontaneous trip or event ahead! You might wake up to packed bags or find yourself at the airport taking a last minute flight. This hiatus is probably related to wellness or exploring or a combination of both even if it is a weird mixture. As long as the heart is happy, so is the soul.

Sunday 11th

It is a day to enjoy but also be careful not to over-indulge, or dramatise, or try to connect to too many people. Every time you turn around there could be another trap. Jupiter's downside of overstepping boundaries, or overdoing things, can show up. Too much of a good thing is a bad thing.

Monday 12th

It is hard to believe, but you might not want to go to work today. Some of you may be lucky and on vacation, but you will also find something that is not the way you like it and throw a temper tantrum or two. Don't take yourself so seriously.

Tuesday 13th

The Sun and Mars are facing each other and the theme of the Full Moon is echoed. Once again, you need to find balance as no side has all the advantages. You are able to take a thorough look at all the details but have to wait to act upon them.

Wednesday 14th

Mercury retrograde is back. There is a deep need to reflect on all the information received, and you turn into an investigative detective to detect what has been hidden. Use the next three weeks for deep conversations with your friends, and they will assist you in getting to the bottom of the situation.

Thursday 15th

The Sun has another discussion with Pluto. It could be a power struggle situation. You could be faced with an authority figure, or you could be the authority figure in charge. In both cases, it is about the fair use of the power that is being wielded. Holding power asks for responsibility and integrity.

Friday 16th

Happy New Moon in Libra! You can set new goals for your career and vocation. The central theme is to retain or establish integrity. How do you want to appear in the world, how do you want to be perceived? How much power do you desire?

Saturday 17th

Your emotions and thoughts align today in the depth of the Scorpio realm. Nothing superficial can touch you, and every answer you find will lead to another question. At least one of your findings will trigger an unexpected emotional response. Either from you or another person. Take that into account.

Sunday 18th

A sense of responsibility, trustworthiness and integrity are some of the values connected to Capricorn. Are you also just, merciful and non-judgemental? Today you might want to ponder how many of these traits you have embodied so far. It is helpful to ask how others perceive you. Your friends can help you reflect on that.

Monday 19th

With a great sense of reality you can estimate how far you can stretch the boundaries, but what happens if you cross them? It can lead to a conflict within your home or an inner conflict regarding your beliefs. You might not want to talk it out but draw back and seek the connection to nature.

Tuesday 20th

From the depths of your subconscious, an old belief might rise to the surface. You might wonder about it or be in a state of disbelief. Remember, whenever you become conscious of something it is an invitation to integrate it as part of yourself. If the belief you have remembered does not serve you – release it.

Wednesday 21st

The right things are starting to happen at the right times. At least sometimes. Venus, in a flowing connection to Pluto, is showing the transformation inside you. You are also integrating the new things that you have learned. It is another stepping stone to the future.

Thursday 22nd

The depth of Scorpio season is knocking on your door, as the Sun is entering your area of friends, communities, hopes and wishes. It is about your deepest desires and with whom you share them. It is about engaging in a trustworthy tribe. Are you willing to dive a little deeper, mountain climber?

Friday 23rd

For you to trust somebody, it is essential that they share your core values. From time to time you should redefine your values, because as you evolve your values shift and change. You might want to discuss your values with your friends, it is very insightful and sometimes surprising.

Saturday 24th

Venus, in a happy conversation with Saturn, makes your heart bloom. You have all the resources ready, the checklist and the building blocks and you are starting to rebuild. Saturn is on its way out of your sign and once he leaves the foundation has to hold steady for the next 30 years.

Sunday 25th

In the darkness there is a light. It is your inner light, and today your mind becomes acquainted with it. To comprehend it entirely you need to allow some time. When you are in the midst of something you often can't see the wood for the trees.

Monday 26th

It could be an emotional day, more emotional than your days usually are. Your imagination can be high and you might be able to focus it outwards, but only if you work and connect with people you know well and feel comfortable with. Avoid working on your own today, there is a tendency for daydreaming.

Tuesday 27th

Do you have high hopes regarding your immediate environment? Are you feeling super comfortable? Is it possible you idealise your circumstances or the comfort it gives? Just feel into this and see if everything really is the way you like it, or if it is just a habit you have learned to love.

Wednesday 28th

Mercury still in retrograde comes back to Libra, like he had forgotten to check on something. Venus is also entering Libra so there is another emphasis on this area. You want to be appreciated in your career and vocational path. What aspect of your public image do you want to re-evaluate?

Thursday 29th

Your emotional focus is on home and family matters and you are willing to take action. There is this need for a work-life balance, and yet the demands are sometimes so conflicting you don't know how to reconcile them. It will take a little longer to work out the solution. Have patience.

Friday 30th

Today is another opportunity to solve conflicts with your family while learning to stand up for yourself and not banging your head against the wall. If you can release more of the beliefs stemming from your childhood, it will become more comfortable every day and allow much healing to take place.

Saturday 31st

A productive spark is waiting to burst out on today's Blue Moon and another side of you is likely to be revealed. Instead of keeping it subdued or locked away in favour of practicalities, as usual, let your mind and imagination wonder. You'll be surprised at what you can create.

117

NOVEMBER

....

Sunday 1st

You want to spend this day in companionship and dedicate it to joy, passion and self-expression. Sudden opportunities wish to be embraced, so you need some flexibility to make the most out of it. There can be a tendency to over-indulge, but snacking is advised.

Monday 2nd

Monday morning and your full hands-on mentality is asked for. You are in your element, focused on the mountaintop and setting one foot in front of the other. Your determination makes others go green with envy, which you might not even notice. Everything is in order, keep going!

Tuesday 3rd

You are busy with all sorts of chores, meetings and calls, and it might feel there is not a minute to pause. It is one of those days when you know you have to take a small time out: stand upright, feet on the ground and breath deep and consciously. Now off you go again.

Wednesday 4th

Time for a happy dance, Mercury retrograde is over!
So in regards to your legacy, what you are aiming for is
likely to be more explicit. You want to set high standards,
and over the coming weeks, you will find the right
people to support you on your future endeavours.

Thursday 5th

Do not forget to invest time in your one-on-one
relationships. When you focus too much on public
demands, you can easily neglect your relationships.
You might get an idea from a business partner to truly
practise equality and fairness in your career path and
become a role model.

Friday 6th

When you take action, you need to stand by your
integrity and be true to who you are. To feel emotionally
safe you need to do it your way. You might come to a
crossroads today and decide which way to go. Go with
Frank and sing: I did it my way.

Saturday 7th

Take another hard look at your resources and the
financial support that can come to you when you
dare to show your full colours. Multiple resources are
available, the question is: are you willing to truly be
yourself? You need to love yourself wholeheartedly in
all aspects to make this possible.

Sunday 8th

There is tension around your ability to shine because there are still things you want to hide away. Have a think about your shadow side, because often it is not only about integrating our darker parts but discovering what light you are hiding out of your own fear to shine.

Monday 9th

As the Moon is coming back to your area of education and vision, you are asked to focus on the essence of your true desires. If you are true to yourself and allow some sense of utopia, what comes to mind? You can take practical steps towards this as nobody but you knows how to make it reality.

Tuesday 10th

Mercury is about to leave the area of vocation and career and comes back to find your tribe and those who can support you on your journey. You now know what legacy you are aiming for and you know who is needed by your side. Your inner detective is back in the game.

Wednesday 11th

A fantastic day to plan, structure and move ahead first and foremost regarding your vision and dreams, and later today also regarding your legacy, which go hand in hand anyway. You can feel how things are moving forward even if it is all at a slow pace, but it is not a race, is it?

Thursday 12th

It is the final meeting of Jupiter and Pluto. You have worked hard on yourself to integrate all aspects of your character and become who you need to be to grow beyond your old limits. Transformation is an ongoing process, and if you focus on your core values, you will always be able to evolve beyond your expectations.

Friday 13th

The energy is getting lower, the days are now darker anyway and to brighten it up you could need the company of your friends. So once work is done, have a meet up, sit at the fireside and have some tea and deep conversations. Chances are you find comfort and some profound truth.

Saturday 14th

Mars retrograde is over, thank goodness. It gave a hard look at your ego, your inner child and the way you stand up for yourself. Your family and the home situation will still remain in focus, but you are now able to do things right and to work out what did not work out before because you changed your perspective.

Sunday 15th

The Scorpio New Moon is a deep and reflective one. You could think it asks you to be on your own, but you can investigate and reflect better while in conversation with the people you want to connect to. Finding your tribe is high on your list.

Monday 16th

So many right questions, opinions and thoughts, your head is still swirling with all the information received. To process you might draw back and seek comfort in nature. With Venus and Jupiter in a discussion, are you conscious what blessings you receive from the outside world? Practise gratitude.

Tuesday 17th

An old belief stored inside of yourself could be that you are not worthy of having fun and need to stick to your responsibilities at all costs. What if you can combine this with fun? Accountability is excellent, and you will be even better if you reserve a spot for joy.

Wednesday 18th

Act from integrity, and you are able to resolve a conflict regarding home and family quickly. This conflict can raise an important question: what action is needed to find the right tribe? Remind yourself what you need to feel emotionally safe. That is the key.

Thursday 19th

Combining your deepest desires with Saturnian determination is a formula of success. You might want to do exactly that today and set another essential building block on your path to mastery. You feel self-confident and deeply connected to your inner core. Somebody is standing loyally by your side, supporting every step you take.

Friday 20th

It is a question of self-worth that determines how much you dare to express yourself. You could be irritated if you receive extensive positive feedback by doing something that you see as rebellious. Chances are that the parts you considered quirky are not so quirky at all or at least very welcome.

Saturday 21st

Two fundamental shifts at once. Venus is entering Scorpio to make sure you set the right boundaries in the relationship with your tribe and friends while the Sun enters Sagittarius and you will find yourself focusing more on your inside and retreat from the outside world. Being in nature is especially important.

Sunday 22nd

With the Moon in Pisces, you enjoy the comfort of your neighbourhood and strolling around near the river. Take some time to listen to water, maybe take a hot coffee or tea with you. Once you are back, allow some time for daydreaming and have your notebook handy to write down your dreams.

Monday 23rd

The Moon is crossing Neptune, so imagination and dream life is vivid. Messages from your subconscious can arise, and you should delay important meetings if you have them. You worked so hard in the last month, really find ways to reduce your working time or go on annual leave during the next few weeks.

Tuesday 24th

The need for reflection and embracing the spirit world is still high. Try to stay at home or leave work early. Starting later would be another option. You might want to dive into a book or a movie to explore a different sense of reality. Messages can hide in a movie, too.

Wednesday 25th

You might be a little impatient today, and there is an urge to take action. Most likely your efforts will relate to your home and family. It is an opportunity to redecorate, rearrange and create a magical atmosphere. Allow some magic to enter your life and feel your inner child jumping with joy.

Thursday 26th

Nurture your inner child to the max! Yes you are grown-up, yes you have responsibilities and duties, but a happy child creates a happy adult. There is lots of power in freeing your inner child and meeting its needs no matter what. Have cocoa, jump around or listen to an audiobook.

Friday 27th

Stick with the inner child and think about what you enjoyed most when you were little. What was fun and had you focused for hours? Try and integrate at least one of these activities back into your life. Mercury and Pluto unlock a treasure, and you recognise how much you have transformed.

Saturday 28th

Imagination still runs high, and you want to keep on embracing joyfulness. The Sun in Sagittarius sparks you with optimism and the time you spend reflecting on yourself is well worth it. Life is beautiful, and you get ready to create new beliefs about the meaning of life.

Sunday 29th

This seems to be a golden week for you, especially if you are allowed to really focus on yourself. You receive new insights from a talk to a friend and feel connected to universal truth. You get excited about the future and might enjoy having an extra special dinner tonight. Just to celebrate life.

Monday 30th

The month ends with the Gemini Full Moon and a partial lunar eclipse. They say eclipses are fated times, and this one asks you to focus on your everyday life. What do you like about it and what do you want it to become? Changes lie ahead, and you are to determine the direction.

125

DECEMBER

....

Tuesday 1st

Are your ready for the finale of 2020? This is no usual
holiday season – it is going to be an intense month
with chapters closing and a massive shift ahead. With
the Moon crossing the north node you feel the future,
and as Mercury comes into Sagittarius, you might want
to write a diary.

Wednesday 2nd

Did you make your first diary entry? It is a fantastic tool
and will assist you in your thoughtful work, and that
will set you up for your future big time. Today you want
to enjoy togetherness and nurture and support your
partner or a close friend.

Thursday 3rd

Remind yourself that giving and taking should be
balanced and that your needs, as well as your partners'
ones, count. Instead of compromises, create win-win
situations that feel nurturing for both of you. Express
your feelings and allow yourself to be vulnerable. This
needs trust but provides for a more profound encounter.

Friday 4th

A question you can ponder and write in your diary today is: how do you want to shine? How do you want to show up and where are you playing a role that is not entirely authentic? Lots of questions but the answers will help to set you up for the future.

Saturday 5th

Your self-expression is linked to the role you see yourself in, and if you get clear about that, you suddenly have a new range of options available. This might also be related to your inner child and how much reassurance you received when you were little.

Sunday 6th

Are you ready for a dreamy Sunday? Your dream could be very vivid as Venus is connecting to Neptune. It is also a Sunday to embrace love. The compassionate, selfless love for the planet, animals and humankind itself and Earthly love too. What is your vision of love?

Monday 7th

Do you have a vision board? It is an excellent time to start one. All you need is a piece of paper, pencils and maybe some photos. Start to picture your wishes and desires in a way that you can express them most naturally. If you do it digitally, print it out to make it more tangible.

Tuesday 8th

It is a fantastic day to make plans, renew your checklists and be pragmatic about the work you do. You are able to focus on work and get your ducks in a row. If you need to prepare stuff for Christmas, it is an excellent opportunity to line things up early.

Wednesday 9th

Be aware, not everything is the way it seems to be today. Be super-honest today especially to yourself. Chances are, a truth revealed can make you feel uncomfortable but not speaking or recognising it would set you out on the wrong path. It is a blessing in disguise.

Thursday 10th

Better safe than sorry. With Venus in Scorpio connecting to Pluto, you are super capable of setting the necessary boundaries and installing a sense of security. Still, something in your perception can be off, but just turn yourself upside down, metaphorically, to see another perspective and have an aha moment.

Friday 11th

Say goodbye to old beliefs today. Take some time for yourself and note down all the beliefs you came across throughout this year. Look especially at those related to your inner child and your parents. Release those that no longer serve you in peace and with a little ritual.

Saturday 12th

The Moon and Venus join, and you might be able to see them together in the morning sky. Meet some friends today and enjoy their company and other than that it is a day to set the course for the future. If you want to install a new habit in your daily routine, start now!

Sunday 13th

This Sunday is just for you Capricorn. Go outside in nature, maybe walking through the snow and tuning into universal truth while you explore your inner world. Make it a sacred day, dedicated to you. It is not a day to get stuff done. If there are things to do, delay them until at least Tuesday.

Monday 14th

Happy New Moon in Sagittarius! This one has a feeling of melancholy attached to it. The old is almost done, new shifts are about to happen, and there is another call to release old and outdated beliefs and replace them with new ones. Life has way more in store for you.

Tuesday 15th

All right. If you have things left on your to-do list, roll up your sleeves and get the job done! If you are in charge, you could also aid others in moving forward with a structure and create very concrete results. The only downside to this energy can be that you might be unstoppable and work on and on.

Wednesday 16th

This is the final time that the Moon finds so many planetary bodies in your sign. You must literally feel the vibration of the change ahead. Take a look in the mirror today and acknowledge yourself for all the changes you've been through, for never giving up and moving on relentlessly.

Thursday 17th

Mark your calendar. There is a huge announcement to make: Saturn is leaving your sign and enters into Aquarius. Your future starts today. It is now all about your self-worth, a new approach to your possessions and your values. It is grounding the vision and creating a new reality.

Friday 18th

Mercury is in the heart of the Sun to receive a message of great importance. As always, allow some time for it to sink in. It is a message about your beliefs and how you want to integrate spirituality in your daily life. Meanwhile, you thrive on the feeling of revolution.

Saturday 19th

Jupiter has his final day in your sign, Capricorn. He liked to guide you, but there was a lot to face. In the upcoming year, Jupiter will help you anchor in the new with more optimism and enthusiasm. Make today a day of gratitude for all the blessings you received in 2020.

Sunday 20th

Just as Jupiter enters Aquarius, it runs into Saturn waiting at the doorstep. When these two meet, there is a new cycle starting. They want to agree on the terms of building this new Earth and reality. You have probably set everything up straight and are ready to go! Exciting!

Monday 21st

Happy Winter Solstice. Everything is going quickly so here is the next major event, a turning of the tides. This is the shortest day and longest night. It is also the return of the light. A vast promise lies within, and surely it is the beginning of your birthday season. Blessings to all Capricorns.

Tuesday 22nd

What is your favourite thing about Christmas? What is your inner child's favourite thing about Christmas? Make sure that you include some of the traditions you love in this year's celebration. If there are last minute changes to be made, take care of them as soon as possible.

131

Wednesday 23rd

Today can indicate power struggles, maybe regarding the preparations for your celebration. The key is to maintain integrity, speak your truth but do everything you can to find a solution. You might need to agree to disagree and stay busy throughout the day, so you have an outlet for all the energy available to you.

Thursday 24th

What a blessing that the Moon enters in the sign of Taurus to ensure a peaceful celebration. You are able to make the final arrangements and have a relaxed evening. Let joy be your anchor point for this year's Christmas celebration and if there are kids involved focus your attention on them.

Friday 25th

Merry Christmas Capricorn! Did Father Christmas fill your stockings? You might find an astonishing gift today that supports your self-expression. Other than that, thoroughly enjoy the day, the board games, running around with the children and eating mince pies and Christmas pudding. Feel the joy and spread the love!

Saturday 26th

Boxing day, boxing day, your dreams are never far away. You still feel like you could sing all the time and today asks you to connect to your imagination. You might want to sit at the fireplace, reading tales, tell your own stories or dive into some movies.

Sunday 27th
Today can feel busy even though it is a Sunday and one could think it is about resting. Not for you, as you want to feel a sense of routine and get lots of chores done, and keep developing new routines. No need to wait for the New Year to start. The time is now.

Monday 28th
The energy is high, the Sun connects to Uranus, and together they set the revolutionising energy free. It is this sense of newness you are happy to create and integrate into your new everyday routine. A considerable part of this new routine is consciously taking breaks and spending some time in nature to recharge.

Tuesday 29th
Happy Full Moon in Cancer. This Full Moon illuminates your relationships. There was a similar Full Moon at the beginning of the year. If you look back now, see how much has changed and how much you could improve your love life by focusing on nurturing yourself. Lots of love for you, Capricorn.

Wednesday 30th

What is love? Is it Earthly love, divine love and universal love? Take your sweetheart by the hand and go for a walk under the starry sky. Let your imagination guide you through the universe and make some wishes. Where do you see your path unfolding together?

Thursday 31st

New Year's Eve is here. 2020 was an intense ride with major cycles coming to a close and new ones that are just beginning. The road ahead is exciting and will feel much lighter. The world needs you and your skills to anchor in the new world. Lead by example.

Capricorn

....

PEOPLE WHO
SHARE YOUR SIGN

PEOPLE WHO SHARE YOUR SIGN

. . . .

Dignified, self-sufficient, and determined, the perseverance and patience of Capricorns makes them often take first place in whatever they set their mind to. Take the King of Rock, Elvis Presley and world-renowned physicist Stephen Hawking as just two examples of what the persevering Capricorn can achieve. Discover which of these established Capricorns share your exact birthday and see if you can spot the similarities.

December 22nd

Meghan Trainor (1993), Shiori Kutsuna (1992), Jordin
Sparks (1989), Chris Carmack (1980), Vanessa Paradis
(1972), Dina Meyer (1968), Ralph Fiennes (1962), Jean-
Michel Basquiat (1960), Héctor Elizondo (1936)

December 23rd

Harry Judd (1985), Jodie Marsh (1978), Corey Haim (1971),
Carla Bruni (1967), Eddie Vedder (1964), Dave Murray
(1956), Carol Ann Duffy (1955), Akihito, Emperor of Japan
(1933), Madam C. J. Walker (1867), Joseph Smith (1805)

December 24th

Louis Tomlinson (1991), Ryan Seacrest (1974), Stephenie
Meyer (1973), Ricky Martin (1971), Ed Miliband (1969),
Kate Spade (1962), Carol Vorderman (1960), Lemmy
Kilmister (1945), Ava Gardner (1922), Howard Hughes
(1905), Empress Elisabeth of Austria (1837)

December 25th

Hailie Jade (1995), Armin van Buuren (1976), Dido (1971),
Justin Trudeau, 23rd Prime Minister of Canada (1971),
Annie Lennox (1954), Sissy Spacek (1949), Jimmy Buffett
(1946), Humphrey Bogart (1899), Muhammad Ali Jinnah,
Founder of Pakistan (1876), Clara Barton (1821)

December 26th
Eden Sher (1991), Andy Biersack (1990), Aaron Ramsey (1990), Kit Harington (1986), Hugo Lloris (1986), Beth Behrs (1985), Alexander Wang (1983), Jared Leto (1971), Lars Ulrich (1963), David Sedaris (1956)

December 27th
Olivia Cooke (1993), Hayley Williams (1988), Lily Cole (1987), Emilie de Ravin (1981), Salman Khan (1965), Gérard Depardieu (1948), John Amos (1939), Marlene Dietrich (1901)

December 28th
Sienna Miller (1981), Noomi Rapace (1979), John Legend (1978), Joe Manganiello (1976), Seth Meyers (1973), Denzel Washington (1954), Maggie Smith (1934), Stan Lee (1922), Woodrow Wilson, 28th US President (1856)

December 29th
Dylan Minnette (1996), Ross Lynch (1995), Kei Nishikori (1989), Alison Brie (1982), Charlotte Riley (1981), Diego Luna (1979), Jude Law (1972), Patricia Clarkson (1959), Ted Danson (1947), Jon Voight (1938)

December 30th

Ellie Goulding (1986), LeBron James (1984), Kristin
Kreuk (1982), Eliza Dushku (1980), Tyrese Gibson
(1978), Tiger Woods (1975), Patti Smith (1946), Rudyard
Kipling (1865)

December 31st

Sam Faiers (1990), PSY (1977), Donald Trump Jr. (1977),
Nicholas Sparks (1965), Val Kilmer (1959), Donna
Summer (1948), John Denver (1943), Ben Kingsley (1943),
Alex Ferguson (1941), Anthony Hopkins (1937), Salman of
Saudi Arabia, King of Saudi Arabia (1935), Henri
Matisse (1869)

January 1st

Jack Wilshere (1992), Colin Morgan (1986), Paolo
Guerrero (1984), Elin Nordegren (1980), Sonali Bendre
(1975), Morris Chestnut (1969), Verne Troyer (1969), J.D.
Salinger (1919), J. Edgar Hoover (1895)

January 2nd

Bryson Tiller (1993), Shelley Hennig (1987), Kate
Bosworth (1983), Dax Shepard (1975), Taye Diggs (1971),
Christy Turlington (1969), Cuba Gooding Jr. (1968),
Tia Carrere (1967)

January 3rd

Danica McKellar (1975), Michael Schumacher (1969),
Mel Gibson (1956), Victoria Principal (1950), Robert
Loggia (1930), Sergio Leone (1929), J. R. R. Tolkien (1892),
Savitribai Phule (1831)

January 4th

Liza Soberano (1998), Toni Kroos (1990), James Milner
(1986), Jeannie Mai (1979), Julia Ormond (1965), Craig
Revel Horwood (1965), Dave Foley (1963), Harlan Coben
(1962), Michael Stipe (1960), Tina Knowles (1954), Rick
Stein (1947)

January 5th

Suki Waterhouse (1992), Kristin Cavallari (1987), Deepika
Padukone (1986), Deadmau5 (1981), January Jones (1978),
Bradley Cooper (1975), Marilyn Manson (1969), Vinnie
Jones (1965), Diane Keaton (1946), Hayao Miyazaki (1941)

January 6th

MattyBRaps (2003), Irina Shayk (1986), Alex Turner
(1986), Kate McKinnon (1984), Eddie Redmayne (1982),
Norman Reedus (1969), Nigella Lawson (1960), Kahlil
Gibran (1883)

January 7th

Eden Hazard (1991), Hardwell (1988), Lewis Hamilton (1985), Lauren Cohan (1982), Vybz Kartel (1976), Jeremy Renner (1971), Irrfan Khan (1967), Nicolas Cage (1964), Christian Louboutin (1963)

January 8th

Noah Cyrus (2000), Sean Paul (1973), David Bowie (1947), Stephen Hawking (1942), Carolina Herrera (1939), Shirley Bassey (1937), Elvis Presley (1935)

January 9th

Nicola Peltz (1995), Nina Dobrev (1989), Kate Middleton, Duchess of Cambridge (1982), Omari Hardwick (1974), Joely Richardson (1965), J. K. Simmons (1955), Jimmy Page (1944), Richard Nixon, 37th U.S. President (1913), Simone de Beauvoir (1908)

January 10th

Abbey Clancy (1986), Jared Kushner (1981), Cash Warren (1979), Jemaine Clement (1974), Maurizio Sarri (1959), Pat Benatar (1953), George Foreman (1949), Rod Stewart (1945)

January 11th

Cody Simpson (1997), Leroy Sané (1996), Jamie Vardy
(1987), Rachel Riley (1986), Amanda Peet (1972), Mary J.
Blige (1971), Kyle Richards (1969), Yolanda Hadid (1964),
Alice Paul (1885)

January 12th

Zayn Malik (1993), Naya Rivera (1987), Raf Simons (1968),
Rob Zombie (1965), Jeff Bezos (1964), Howard Stern
(1954), Kirstie Alley (1951), Haruki Murakami (1949),
Swami Vivekananda (1863)

January 13th

Liam Hemsworth (1990), Julian Morris (1983), Ruth
Wilson (1982), Orlando Bloom (1977), Michael Peña
(1976), Nicole Eggert (1972), Patrick Dempsey (1966), Julia
Louis-Dreyfus (1961), Janet Hubert (1956)

January 14th

Grant Gustin (1990), Yandel (1977), Jason Bateman (1969),
Dave Grohl (1969), LL Cool J (1968), Zakk Wylde (1967),
Carl Weathers (1948), Holland Taylor (1943)

January 15th
Dove Cameron (1996), Skrillex (1988), Kelly Kelly (1987),
Ben Shapiro (1984), Pitbull (1981), Regina King (1971),
Shane McMahon (1970), Martin Luther King Jr. (1929)

January 16th
FKA twigs (1988), Nick Valensi (1981), Lin-Manuel
Miranda (1980), Aaliyah (1979), Kate Moss (1974),
Roy Jones Jr. (1969), John Carpenter (1948), René
Angélil (1942)

January 17th
Calvin Harris (1984), Ray J (1981), Zooey Deschanel (1980),
Tiësto (1969), Michelle Obama (1964), Jim Carrey (1962),
Muhammad Ali (1942), James Earl Jones (1931), Betty
White (1922), Al Capone (1899)

January 18th
Karan Brar (1999), Kelly Rohrbach (1990), Angelique
Kerber (1988), Jason Segel (1980), Pep Guardiola (1971),
Dave Bautista (1969), Mark Rylance (1960), Kevin Costner
(1955), Cary Grant (1904)

January 19th

Logan Lerman (1992), Mac Miller (1992), Claudio
Marchisio (1986), Utada Hikaru (1983), Jenson Button
(1980), Ricardo Arjona (1964), Dolly Parton (1946), Janis
Joplin (1943), Edgar Allan Poe (1809)

January 20th

Evan Peters (1987), Joe Swash (1982), Mark Wright (1981),
Gary Barlow (1971), Stacey Dash (1967), Rainn Wilson
(1966), Bill Maher (1956), Paul Stanley (1952), David Lynch
(1946), Dorothy Provine (1935), Tom Baker (1934), Buzz
Aldrin (1930), Federico Fellini (1920)